Twayne's New Critical Introductions
to Shakespeare

By the same author

Shakespeare: The Winter's Tale (London: Edward Arnold, 1966).
Two Concepts of Allegory: A Study of Shakespeare's The Tempest *and the Logic of Allegorical Expression* (London: Routledge & Kegan Paul, 1967).
A Common Sky: Philosophy and the Literary Imagination (London: Chatto & Windus for Sussex University Press, 1974).
Milton: The Minor Poems in English, introduction, pp. 17–60 (London: Macmillan, 1972).
Dostoevsky's Crime and Punishment*: Murder as Philosophic Experiment* (Edinburgh: Scottish Academic Press for Sussex University Press, 1978).
Overheard by God: Fiction and Prayer in Herbert, Milton and St John (London: Methuen, 1980).
A New Mimesis: Shakespeare and the Representation of Reality (London: Methuen, 1983).
Pope's Essay on Man (London: George Allen & Unwin, 1984).

Twayne's New Critical Introductions to Shakespeare

TIMON OF ATHENS

A.D. Nuttall

Fellow of New College, Oxford

TWAYNE PUBLISHERS · BOSTON

A Division of G. K. Hall & Co.

Published in the United States by Twayne Publishers,
division of G. K. Hall & Co.,
70 Lincoln Street, Boston, Massachusetts.

Published simultaneously in Great Britain by
Harvester Wheatsheaf
66 Wood Lane End, Hemel Hempstead, Herts.

Twayne's New Critical Introductions to Shakespeare, no. 8

Library of Congress Cataloging-in-Publication Data

Nuttall, A. D. (Anthony David)
Timon of Athens.
(Twayne's new critical introductions to Shakespeare)
Bibliography: p.
1. Shakespeare, William, 1564–1616. Timon of Athens.
I. title. II. Series.
PR2834.N88 1989 822.3'3 89-2005
ISBN 0-8057-8714-3
ISBN 0-8057-8715-1 (pbk.)

To John Batchelor and Emrys Jones

Titles in the Series

GENERAL EDITOR: GRAHAM BRADSHAW

Jane Adamson	*Troilus and Cressida*
Graham Bradshaw	*Henry IV*
Maurice Charney	*Titus Andronicus*
S. L. Goldberg	*Antony and Cleopatra*
Harriett Hawkins	*Measure for Measure*
Alexander Leggatt	*King Lear*
Michael Long	*Macbeth*
John Lyon	*The Merchant of Venice*
Tom McCavera	*The Tempest*
A. D. Nuttall	*Timon of Athens*
Adrian Poole	*Coriolanus*
Wilbur Sanders	*The Winter's Tale*
Cedric Watts	*Hamlet*
Sheldon Zitner	*All's Well That Ends Well*

General Editor's Preface

The *New Critical Introductions to Shakespeare* series will include studies of all Shakespeare's plays, together with two volumes on the non-dramatic verse, and is designed to offer a challenge to all students of Shakespeare.

Each volume will be brief enough to read in an evening, but long enough to avoid those constraints which are inevitable in articles and short essays. Each contributor will develop a sustained critical reading of the play in question, which addresses those difficulties and critical disagreements which each play has generated.

Different plays present different problems, different challenges and excitements. In isolating these, each volume will present a preliminary survey of the play's stage history and critical reception. The volumes then provide a more extended discussion of these matters in the main text, and of matters relating to genre, textual problems and the use of source material, or to historical and theoretical issues. But here, rather than setting a row of dragons at the gate, we have assumed that 'background' should figure only as it emerges into a critical foreground; part of the critical endeavour is to establish, and sift, those issues which seem most pressing.

So, for example, when Shakespeare determined that *his* Othello and Desdemona should have no time to live together, or that Cordelia dies while Hermione survives, his deliberate departures from his source material have a critical significance which is often blurred, when discussed in the context of lengthily detailed surveys of 'the sources'. Alternatively, plays like *The Merchant of Venice* or *Measure for Measure* show Shakespeare welding together different 'stories' from quite different sources, so that their relation to each other becomes a matter for critical debate. And Shakespeare's dramatic practice poses different critical questions when we ask – or if we ask: few do – why particular characters in a poetic drama speak only in verse or only in prose; or when we try to engage with those recent, dauntingly specialised and controversial textual studies which set out to establish the evidence for authorial revisions or joint authorship. We all read *King Lear* and *Macbeth*, but we are not all textual critics; nor are textual critics always able to show where their arguments have critical consequences which concern us all.

Just as we are not all textual critics, we are not all linguists, cultural anthropologists, psychoanalysts or New Historicists. The diversity of contemporary approaches to Shakespeare is unprecedented, enriching, bewildering. One aim of this series is to represent what is illuminating in this diversity. As the hastiest glance through the list of contributors will confirm, the series does not attempt to 'reread' Shakespeare by placing an ideological grid over the text and reporting on whatever shows through. Nor would the series' contributors always agree with each other's arguments, or premisses; but each has been invited to develop a sustained critical argument which will also provide its own critical and historical context – by taking account of those issues which have perplexed or divided audiences, readers, and critics past and present.

Graham Bradshaw

Contents

Preface

It will be said that this book smells more of the study than of the theatre. Yet it began with a theatrical experience. In 1980 I saw Richard Pasco play the part of Timon at the Other Place in Stratford. It was an immensely exciting performance, operating equally on the emotions and the intellect (which perhaps suggests that we ought not, after all, to draw too absolute a distinction between the study and the theatre). I was unable to sleep afterwards, haunted both by the image of a stricken human face and by certain obstinate paradoxes which had fastened on my mind. Years later, after I had completed this study, I came upon Richard Pasco's essay on playing Timon in *Players of Shakespeare*, edited by Philip Brockbank (Cambridge: Cambridge University Press, 1985, pp. 129–38). To read this admirable essay was for me a curious experience; it suggested that my debt to the original performance may have been greater than I knew. Richard Pasco observes in his essay both that we hear nothing of any wife, son or daughter in the play and that Timon is, of all Shakespeare's major figures, the most alone. Both of these observations I had thought of as, in some sense, my own property (not because unprecedented in the writings of others, but because they were both, as it seemed, the warm material of personal, literary discovery). It is in fact obviously possible – or even probable – that they were planted in my mind by that astonishingly intelligent, principled performance.

I am very grateful to Emrys Jones, who read and commented on my typescript (the errors and absurdities which remain are of course all mine), and to Margaret Whitlock for typing – with enormous skill and unfailing good humour – a vilely written manuscript.

A. D. Nuttall
New College, Oxford

ACKNOWLEDGEMENTS

All references to *Timon of Athens* are to the New Arden edition by H. J. Oliver (London: Methuen, 1963, corrected reprint of the 1959 edition). All other references to Shakespeare are to *The Riverside Shakespeare* (Boston: Houghton Mifflin, 1974).

I do not always follow lover, elder brother and woman;
sometime the philosopher.

The Stage History

No record survives of any performance of *Timon of Athens* during the period before the theatres were closed by the Long Parliament in 1642. That the play must nevertheless have had some impact before that date is strongly suggested by Richard Brome's *The City Wit* (not printed until 1653). In this play the formerly liberal, now ruined hero, Crasy, applies to his friends for aid and is snubbed.[1] In 1678 Betterton played Timon in a performance given by the Duke's company at their Dorset Garden Theatre. Purcell is known to have composed music for a performance of *Timon* in 1694.[2] By this time adaptations had begun to appear, of which the most successful was Shadwell's *Timon of Athens, the Man-Hater*. This was staged over and over again through the first four decades of the eighteenth century, and was at last revised in its turn by Richard Cumberland in 1771. But we have no account of a performance of Shakespeare's play in England at any time in the eighteenth century (although we know of a performance in Dublin in 1761).[3] There is a notable asymmetry between this featureless tract of stage history and a not unimportant period of critical interpretation, since the eighteenth century produces the model by which *Timon* may be read as an exemplum of the dangers of ostentatious liberality, later countered in the nineteenth century by the Romantic picture of Timon the idealist.

In 1816 Leigh Hunt wrote a critical report in *The Examiner* of the 'restored' *Timon*, presented by the

Honourable George Lamb; the restoration, it emerges, was less than complete since the courtesans were removed.[4] Samuel Phelps's productions at Sadler's Wells in 1851 and 1856 amazed with their elaborately antiquarian sets (by Fenton). Charles Calvert produced the play in Manchester in 1871, playing Timon himself. A better actor (?), Benson, appears to have had worse luck with a performance at Stratford in 1892. Nevertheless Benson's version was the basis for J. H. Leigh's production (the first of the twentieth century) at the Court Theatre in 1904. His 'slightly gauche' Timon (*The Times*, 19 May 1904) sounds interesting today, but of course may not have been. An Old Vic production followed in 1922, with Robert Atkins producing, and then a thin scattering of performances: one at the Greenhill Street picture house in 1928, Tyrone Guthrie's at the Maddermarket Theatre in 1933 and Nugent Monk's at the Westminster Theatre in 1935.[5] For this last, a young Benjamin Britten wrote the music. Willard Stoker's Birmingham Repertory Theatre production of 1947 was, most adventurously, in modern dress. In 1952 Guthrie tried another production, this time with the Old Vic, casting André Morell as Timon and Leo McKern as Apemantus. The Old Vic's third *Timon* was produced in 1956 by Michael Benthall, with Sir Ralph Richardson in the leading role.

The most talked-about body of performances of *Timon* in the twentieth century must be those given by G. Wilson Knight, beginning with solo versions, first in Toronto and then in Leeds, in the 1940s. The really astonishing performance was given at the Northcott Theatre in Exeter in November 1975. On this occasion Knight's ultra-Romantic conception of Timon as Shakespeare's most starkly, most suddenly tragic hero was pushed to a kind of limit, with the 78-year-old actor, upon the words 'Well, sir, I will' (v. i. 167), discarding almost all his clothes. The whole sequence remains so baffling that it seems wisest simply to give Knight's own stage direction and comment: 'Timon loosens his loin-cloth and holds it dangling in his left hand. Lights lower slightly or are concentrated with shadows. Timon wears a gold sex-covering.' 'Gold here suggests Timon's supersexuality, his status as a 'Phoenix'-type.'[6] Four years earlier Peter Brook directed a French version of the play at the Théâtre des Bouffes-du-Nord in Paris.[7] Of the more recent productions, by far the most important to the writer of this book is that given at the Other Place in Stratford in 1980, in which Richard Pasco played the lead. But this I have already described in my Preface.

The Critical Reception

We think naturally of Shakespeare as the poet of plenitude. Where others husband their resources, keeping the reader alive (but only just), he gives abundantly. But in *Timon of Athens* Shakespeare chose to write in a different mode. In this play he deliberately starves the reader (for the moment I shall use 'reader' to cover both 'auditor' and 'reader-of-text', since even in a theatre the process of apprehension is less instantaneous, more structured than is commonly supposed). Humane richness, psychological complexity, warmth of relationship – all factors which promote audience-identification – are to some extent withheld. Timon, like Lear, is the victim of ingratitude, but, unlike Lear, never learns charity and has no wife or child to love or be grieved by. Even Molière's Alceste had his love for Célimène, but in *Timon of Athens* the drama is purged of all natural relations of affection, leaving instead the cold structures of an extreme yet somehow vacuous liberality, succeeded by an inhuman and therefore unsympathetic misanthropy. Late in the play Apemantus tells Timon, 'The middle of humanity thou never knewest, but the extremity of both ends' (IV. iii. 301). What is true of the protagonist is also true, in a manner, of the play itself. The opulent middle ground of common humanity is abandoned; the dramatist has, for certain special purposes of meditation and probation, chosen to pitch his tent in a kind of wilderness. But none of this – though the enterprise carries the risk of artistic suicide – is fundamentally incompatible with the exercise of dramatic and poetic art. Shakespeare (perhaps with a little help from friends) here dramatises inhumanity itself and in doing so explores, as the proper formal correlative of such a venture, a distinctively Renaissance alienation effect (having links with the stiff archaic formalism of Greek tragedy, less coarsely assertive than Brechtian *Verfremdungseffekt* but sharing therewith an interest in holding off audience empathy). It is a play which has won few friends, but then it does not conciliate affection.

How, it may be asked, is so bloodless a drama to live? I answer: it lives first in the expectation of warmth (for generosity and ingratitude are in themselves themes of powerful emotional import) and then, as that expectation is defeated and the disturbing interconnectedness of high-minded morality and base economic relations gradually exposed, it lives in the intelligence.

No one knows when *Timon of Athens* was written, but its style strongly suggests 1607/8 as a likely date. It would then belong to the 'Plutarchian' transitional period between the great tragedies (*King Lear*, *Macbeth*) and the late romances. It may be that *Antony and Cleopatra*, in which indeed we find lyrical richness, was succeeded by the more austere *Coriolanus*, which was followed in its turn by the harshest of them all, *Timon*. *As You Like It*, to which (because it contains a misanthrope) frequent reference will be made in this book, belongs to an earlier phase of Shakespeare's art (1599).

The history of the critical reception of *Timon of Athens* has been told by Francelia Butler in her book, *The Strange Critical Fortunes of Shakespeare's Timon of Athens*. Those who assume that critical hostility to the initial generosity of Timon is an exclusively modern reaction will be surprised to learn that in the eighteenth century he was regarded as a fool and a spendthrift. The critic of the *General Evening Post*, writing in 1772, finds the play sub-tragic precisely because we cannot pity its principal figure: 'We consider him as a blockhead very properly undone by his extravagance, and even rejoice in his sufferings as in the natural execution of poetic justice.'[1] One senses in this passage that informed opinion may be hardening, and, at the same time, growing simpler. As early as 1698 Edward Filmer (if it was he) had, in his defence of Shakespeare against Collier's attack, achieved a surprisingly subtle and balanced view, finding the play fully tragic because, although we despise the prodigal, we pity the misanthrope.[2] William Richardson wrote in 1783, 'Real goodness is not ostentatious. Not so is the goodness of Timon . . .. Timon is not more ostentatious, impatient of admonition, desirous of applause, injudicious in gifts and undistinguishing in his choice of friends, than he is profuse.'[3] But it may be that in the eighteenth century, as in the twentieth, audiences were more willing than critics to sympathise, for Richardson adds, 'This is not the view usually entertained.'[4] It seems that theatre-goers (who were by this period seeing not Shakespeare's play but variously creative adaptations of it) especially enjoyed the railing of Timon and Apemantus. In 1770 one Paul Hiffernan produced an elaborate proposal for a temple to Shakespeare, as eloquent in its way of the taste of the age as are the statues which stand to this day in Stratford-upon-Avon of a later phase. He places Timon, curiously, in the *comic* sequence of images, between Touchstone and Rosalind, on the one side, and Shylock and Portia on the other – Timon to be shown with Apemantus, 'railing at each other'.[5]

In the nineteenth century the picture changes: Timon is glorified as the Noble Spirit. Hazlitt, indeed, in an admirable essay (1817), was careful to set forth the first part of the play in terms of pomp and profusion rather than of love,[6] but Swinburne, some sixty years later, has no reservations: he ascribes to Timon an 'immeasurable superiority in spiritual rank to the hermit fathers of the desert'.[7]

The twentieth century has seen a revival of the sceptical attitude. Willard Farnham, L. C. Knights and Derek

Traversi have variously exposed the frailties of a hero once more seen as flawed.[8] H. J. Oliver and J. C. Maxwell in the introductions to their distinguished editions of the play both in a manner revert to the position of our earliest critic, Filmer: we pity Timon despite his faults. The grand exception is Wilson Knight, who in a manner revived the nineteenth-century perception of this work. Like Hazlitt, Knight brings out the impetus of the play, its singleness, the completeness of the change, the intensity of the whole. At the same time, however, Knight transformed Shakespearean criticism, roughly speaking, by foregrounding image patterns over disquisitions on character and plot. Where before we had said, '*Macbeth* is about a man who seized the crown of Scotland', we learned to say, '*Macbeth* is darkness and blood'. The sense of seizing the essence of the work is immensely increased. This book, as will become obvious, is a kind of running argument with the work of Wilson Knight. Although I disagree with him so much, I have no doubt of his stature. For me, his simple picture of the lover of mankind succeeded by the hater will not do, backed though it is by a dazzling command of corroborative images. Part of my case against Knight is that this is, at its root, an intellectual play and is therefore made out of thoughts as well as images. It is not enough to imagine gold; one must think about money. The complex relational notion of *obligation*, with its ramifying patterns, is as central to the play as is the image of the dog. This does not mean that I take the play to be a philosophical treatise. The overall pattern which results, though it moves majestically to a kind of synthesis, is designedly discordant, relishing the posing of questions more than the achievement of solutions. It is true that the play presents a moral theorem, a paradigmatic change of fortune, with a simplicity which has reminded many scholars of the late-medieval Morality Play, but in *Timon of Athens* this very simplicity is registered, within the play, as strange. Its starkness is made to serve an aesthetic end. We realise that we are not after all in the Middle

Ages. I am aware, as all who write on this harsh, mannered play must be, of the brilliant work of M. C. Bradbrook. I owe much to the twentieth-century emphasis, by John W. Draper, A. S. Collins, E. C. Pettit and Kenneth Muir, on economics and the decay of 'feudal morality'. But I owe most to the man with whom I disagree.

Timon of Athens is not, to put it mildly, a polished piece; but its intellectual movement is indeed almost Euclidian. Emrys Jones speaks accurately of its 'conceptual magnificence'.[9] The play is like a procession, sculptured in relief, to be apprehended serially before the underlying intellectual structure is realised in the mind. I have therefore chosen in this essay to work through the successive figures or postures of the drama, before turning to the heart of the work, which I take to be its central parodic version of the eucharistic feast.

It will be evident that, although I grant that *Timon* is an untidy, ill-finished piece of work, I do not concede that it is a bad play. Scholars have fallen with delight upon the technical problems thrown up by the ragged text, but the literary critics have hung back, as if repelled in equal measure by the unbalanced, inhuman misanthropy of the hero and by the unbalanced, inhuman generosity which precedes it. None of this is, I submit, the result of authorial inadvertence or incompetence. This is the strangest of all Shakespeare's tragedies. If we are to understand both the special austerity of this play and its oddly violent emotion, we must read with a new sort of attention.

Part 1

The Succession of Figures

· 1 ·

The *Paragone*

Timon of Athens, as printed in the Folio of 1623 (the sole authoritative text), reaches us from the first as a curiously *readerly* work of art. I now use 'readerly' in its most specific sense; I mean that we seem to be confronted by something which exists, most crucially, on the page, rather than – say – in the implied stage performance. There is a loose association in many people's minds of the theatrical with the untidy and, conversely, of the readerly with the deliberately polished composition. We think perhaps of *Samson Agonistes* (never intended to the stage, as Milton said) as against *Doctor Faustus*, a play smelling equally of brimstone and grease-paint. But *Timon of Athens* is certainly not tidy. Many scholars have inferred from the various loose ends and inconsistencies that it is unfinished. Yet as soon as one takes up the book one is aware of an autonomous object, squarely confronting the literate eye. Before the opening words of dialogue we have the stage direction, 'Enter Poet, Painter, Jeweller, Merchant and Mercer, at severall doores'. The effect of this is both immediate and distinctive. It is quite different, for example, from 'Enter Pandarus and Troylus' or 'Enter a Company of Mutinous Citizens, with Staves, Clubs and other weapons'. These are the normal, functional stage directions of the developed Elizabethan theatre. In contrast, the opening words of the *Timon* text, with categories in place of individual names or dynamic description, are faintly reminiscent of the Morality. Yet we know from the title, backed up by the classicising parade of 'Actus Primus. Scaena Prima' (presumably the work of an editor), that we are firmly placed in the Renaissance. In consequence, even before one has read a line of dialogue, the stage direction has created (though very faintly) an effect of mannered alienation. The anonymous persons of the opening scene are presented, so to speak, colourlessly: in profile, as in some ancient frieze. W. B. Yeats, who once entitled a poem 'Certain Artists bring her Dolls and Drawings', clearly understood the special aesthetic of exclusion I am trying to characterise. The ordinary signals of humanity or individuality are withheld. Instead we have a schematic, graven clarity – or rather the appearance of clarity, for this is not, as I have already suggested and as will be more and more obvious as we go on, a long-laboured, polished work of art. The Mercer, to the embarrassment of modern editors, seems to be superfluous, for (unless he rather than the Merchant is one of the speakers marked 'Mer.') he plays no part whatever in the scene and is accordingly excised from most modern editions.

So far none of this exists in the theatrical experience, though a fairly stylised manner of performance might provide an equivalent effect. In general, however, we must say that any such impression will be formed more gradually. In the theatre we see various unnamed persons and then, from words and signals, pick up, in a thoroughly human fashion, who or what they are. This, the theatrical version, it will be said, is the proper, the *real* experience of the play. Yet the reader's experience also, indisputably, exists. *Julius Caesar* opens, in the Folio, with 'Enter Flavius, Marullus, and certaine Commoners over the Stage'. Here, after the proper names of individuals, we have the minimally functional description, 'certaine Commoners', which is closely in line with what the audience will have inferred already, before the first speech has been delivered. The opening speeches, with efficient swiftness, then inform the audience of the trades of those present ('Speak, what trade art thou?' 'Why, Sir, a Carpenter', and so on). Thus in *Julius Caesar* the *theatrical* categorisation of the persons as they enter is actually slightly more rapid and explicit than in *Timon of Athens*. The stage direction in *Julius Caesar* is thoroughly deferential to the theatrical values: it implicitly warns the reader that the play exists more fully on the stage than on the page. But the first words of Timon are, as we have seen, assertively bookish – one can almost say, 'printerly'.

But of course the stage directions may not be authorial. If this one is not so then it is perhaps just a lucky accident that the first chord struck, for the reader, is in the long run corroborated by the play which follows. For *Timon of Athens* as a whole is a play of warring categories, deliberately stylised. In fact, however, the stage directions of *Timon* look very much as if they are authorial. More than thirty years ago W. W. Greg observed:

> From a study of the stage-directions that may reasonably be supposed to have originated in the author's own manuscript it appears that they commonly wrote many that could be of no immediate help to the prompter, but which describe a scene as they imagine it when writing, and which could at best, as Chambers remarks, serve the company in the production of the play. In their evocative quality many of the directions have, indeed, a literary appeal, as though they were written for the reader rather than the actor. This too is natural enough, for a play was, as a rule, read to the company and had to secure approval before it was accepted, and the more readily and vividly it could be followed the better its chances would be.[1]

Greg includes in his list of 'descriptive directions' the famous one of *Timon*, I. ii. 1, 'Then comes dropping after all Apemantus discontentedly like himself'.[2] Almost as vivid though briefer is the description of the Lords at I. ii. 142: 'The Lords rise from Table with much adoring of [i.e. homage to] Timon.' This last is not cited by Greg, but he does cite as 'authorial-descriptive' a marvellously anonymous, 'profile' stage direction at *3 Henry VI*, II. v. 55: 'Enter a Sonne that hath kill'd his Father, at one doore: and a Father that hath kill'd his Sonne at another doore.'[3] This, notice, has, together with its descriptive vividness, the quality of alienation which first arrested us in *Timon*.

The play proper begins with an exchange of courtesies, after which the focus is successively narrowed. The Poet asks how the world goes and hears in effect that, in a general way, it gets worse and worse. He then asks (in precious, tumid verse) to be told of wonders, pausing in the course of his request to register the presence of the Merchant and the Jeweller. The Merchant (now we begin to 'home in') comes within earshot, praising some unnamed person (in fact Timon, as we soon learn), but his elaborate discourse, almost as elegant as the Poet's, is itself broken in upon by an obtrusion of the concrete – in a highly marketable form. It goes like this:

Mer. A most incomparable man, breath'd, as it were,
To an untirable and continuate goodness.
He passes.
Jew. I have a jewel here –
Mer. O pray, let's see't. For the Lord Timon, Sir?
(I. i. 10–13)

The Merchant's phrase, 'He passes', is usually glossed as 'He excels' or 'He surpasses', and an absolute use of the verb is postulated, in line with the adjective 'passing'. This is certainly possible Shakespearean English. George Page in *The Merry Wives of Windsor* twice remonstrates with the insensate Ford, 'This passes!', meaning 'This is too much!' (IV. ii. 122 and 137). But it is also just possible that the Merchant was about to employ the commoner idiom, 'He passes praise', or the like, and was *interrupted* by the Jeweller, whereupon he not only happily acquiesces in the interruption but himself in turn interrupts the

Jeweller (his disinterested panegyric of Timon now forgotten) to demand a closer look. Once he has had his look his thought indeed reverts to Timon, but now in a patently interested fashion. We learn at once from the Jeweller that the stone is indeed for Timon, but only if he will, in effect, pay a suitable price. The whole exchange, with its overlapping technique, is a very ordinary piece of Jacobean writing. There is no great excitement, no startling language or metaphor as yet, but the author is deftly arranging our minds and expectations in preparation for what is to come.

Immediately upon his rapid *diminuendo* from the generous to the self-interested, the Poet solemnly affirms,

> When we for recompense have prais'd the wild,
> It stains the glory in that happy verse
> Which áptly sings the good.
>
> (I. i. 14–16)

The New Arden editor, after some hesitation, rejects the usual view that these lines are from some poem which the Poet is either reading aloud or reciting; instead he marks the speech as an 'aside'. But the Poet's words at line 20, 'A thing slipp'd idly from me', tend to confirm the received interpretation. Moreover we do not want – or Shakespeare does not want – these particular characters to be *too* morally aware of their ultimate situation at this stage in the play; better the half-inadvertent shrewdness of a general literary observation which perhaps hits the nail more squarely on the head than the Poet knows. Certainly the elevated moral reflection has no effect on the Merchant, who continues to scrutinise the jewel in a professionally expert manner. This is less funny if the Poet's words are treated as an 'aside', inaudible to the Merchant.

The Poet does seem, however, to be interested in other things, apart from jewels. He is interested, for example, in poetry – or in the genesis of poetry ('Our poetry is a gum which oozes / From whence 't is nourish'd', I. i. 21–2) – or else, we at last begin to see, in himself. We are at once presented with a pretty play of egotisms, dressed up as courtesies. The Painter, for his part, offers a marvellous oscillation between self-aggrandisement and self-disparagement.

Pet. Let's see your piece.
Pain. 'Tis a good piece.
Poet. So 'tis; this comes off well and excellent.
Pain. Indifferent.
Poet. Admirable . . .

(I. i. 28–30)

The Painter is almost wrong-footed by the Poet. He begins in insecurity and therefore praises his own piece, a little too strongly. The Poet courteously agrees and 'ups' the praise. Then the Painter, realising that he is safe after all, clumsily swings over in his nervousness to the disparaging 'indifferent'. Several lines of vacuous praise from the Poet must elapse before the Painter can recover equilibrium with 'it is a pretty mocking of this life', where pretty is at once an approving and a minimising word.

As the Senators crowd in to call upon Timon, the Poet, who is an altogether more confident character than the Painter, warms to the theme of his own genius:

I have in this rough work shap'd out a man,
Whom this beneath world doth embrace and hug
With amplest entertainment. My free drift
Halts not particularly, but moves itself
In a wide sea of wax: no levell'd malice
Infects one comma in the course I hold,
But flies an eagle flight, bold, and forth on,
Leaving no tract behind.

(I. i. 42–50)

Now, as the poetry begins to stir, the thought also quickens, becomes more challenging and difficult. The 'wide sea of wax' is a major editorial crux. The basic sense would seem to be that the poet's gift is so far-ranging that it cannot be confined within a single tablet of wax but rather moves freely over oceanic surfaces (as if one were to say in the twentieth century, 'An A4 pad is not enough for me; I need oceans of paper'). It is just possible that Shakespeare began to worry that the account of literary publication at I. i. 26 was a shade too modern even for a highly notional ancient Athens and therefore sought to get in some chronological local colour in the shape of wax tablets and styluses. If so his success is surely doubtful; almost no one in the audience would have understood, the expression being so elliptical.

At this point what began as a flurry of courtesies between two 'territorially conscious' individuals begins to take on the more impersonal atmosphere of the *Paragone*. This was a formalised controversy in Renaissance Italy about the status of the painter in society, especially in relation to that of the poet.[4] Lucian, whose Greek dialogue *Timon, the Misanthrope* is a likely source for Shakespeare's play, tells us in another work how he hesitated as a child between a career as a sculptor (following family tradition and his own more obvious aptitude) and a career as a man of letters. In telling the story he includes a mildly bizarre detail: he ingeniously turned his wax tablets (the working tool of the literary man) into a means of plastic modelling; he scraped the wax off each tablet and, when he had enough, he made from it little figures of cows, horses, men and women.[5]

There is no reason to suppose that Shakespeare read the *Somnium* of Lucian but it does look as if his mind was caught by the fact that wax is employed in literary composition yet is itself plastic, physical. In v. iii the Soldier who finds Timon's epitaph graven on the tomb in the woods determines, because he cannot read the learned script or language in which it is written, to take an impression of the letters with wax (v. iii. 6). In the next scene we are again told about the waxen impression of the words, but this time the language is more lyrically alive:

My noble general, Timon is dead,
Entomb'd upon the very hem o' th' sea;

> And on his gravestone this insculpture which
> With wax I brought away, whose soft impression
> Interprets for my poor ignorance.
>
> (v. iv. 65–9)

Here, as in the crux at I. i. 47, the word 'wax' occurs close to the word 'sea'. In the later passage the poetry is working strongly with notions of hardness and softness, and then with formlessness. The hardness of the inscription, incised in stone, reappears in the softer medium of wax, and meanwhile the liquid sea begins to encroach upon it. Timon told us himself that he had 'made his everlasting mansion / Upon the beached verge of the salt flood, / Who once a day with his embossed froth / The turbulent surge shall cover' (v. i. 214–17). We have run ahead to that part of the play in which all structures, even the structures of hatred, are beginning to dislimn, to lapse into nothingness. We may remember how, when Timon's household breaks up, the Steward says, 'We must all part / Into this sea of air' (IV. ii. 21–2). The Soldier's speech returns us to the notion of interpretation which is, in a manner, to re-evoke the original preoccupation of the Poet in I. i with poetry itself. We need to remember that the Poet is meditating a work which will in some degree pre-echo the story of Timon himself and therefore the play before us (I. i. 65–95). The Poet's project is at once clairvoyant and uncomprehending (and this in its turn may remind us of Shakespeare's Richard II, his 'poet king').

Shakespearean drama continually exhibits such intricate coherencies and transformations. That they should be traceable even in a careless or unfinished composition like *Timon of Athens* strongly suggests that they were native to him, were the way his mind worked. In pursuing them we have moved from the relative certainty of our original lexical comment (that the 'crux' is an allusion to the ancient practice of writing on wax tablets) to less determinate nuances of implication and association.

In this secondary area there is more – much more – to be said. It is probably relevant that *wax* also means 'swell' or 'increase' (as with a waxing moon). Further, we need to remember that Jacobeans wrote with plumes, or feathers, and that archers fledged their arrows with feathers (compare French *flèche*). The plume or pen is implicit throughout the passage and the archer taking aim is hinted in 'levell'd' at line 47. The New Arden editor says 'aimed as one aims a gun', but surely, if we are to be alive to the myriad buried connections of poetry, we should think of a bowman rather than a gunner. This brings us to the eagle, which is now, so to speak, freed from its link with the pen by being launched into the trackless air. The pen leaves a trace, a mark, but the Poet's eagle-flight is bolder, 'leaving no tract behind' (I. i. 50). The wax tablet became the illimitable sea; now the sea becomes sky.

We sense, however, that even as the material links begin to break up a new mythical pattern is beginning to form. Here Edward A. Armstrong brilliantly lit upon the key to its meaning, which is Icarus. He wrote:

> In the background of the poet's thought is Icarus, who attached wings to his back with wax and for whom pride came before a fall. He also comes under the master idea Pride and is naturally linked with the image cluster in which the eagle appears.[6]

This must be right and yet the reference of the myth is puzzling. It is as if the idea is too strong for the (unimpressive) Poet who is struggling to apply it to himself – as if, really, it applies elsewhere. It takes us in fact to Timon himself. For the play *Timon* runs on two simultaneous myths, one favouring, the other undermining the hero. The favouring myth is the one projected by the Poet at I. i. 61–95. It is all about munificence answered by ingratitude. The undermining myth is about excess and showing off, and the fall which follows such displays. When the idea of borrowed feathers turns up later in the play it is firmly applied to Timon himself:

> When every feather sticks in his own wing,
> Lord Timon will be left a naked gull,
> Which flashes now a phoenix.
>
> (II. i. 30–2)

The same image may be present, vestigially and altogether more loosely, in the Fool's random sexual jibes at II. ii. 71. In answer to the civil enquiry, 'How does your mistress?' he says, 'She's e'en setting on water to scald such chickens as you are.' The broad reference is to venereal disease, the narrower to plucking chickens (one scalds a chicken to make the feathers come out more easily).

If the Icarus figure is really Timon we have in this speech a curious phenomenon of counter-infiltration. The Poet more or less unconsciously pre-empts the play in which he figures by conceiving, proleptically, a parallel fiction; but when he seeks mythically to describe the flight of his own clairvoyant invention he ends by inadvertently describing not himself but Timon. Moreover, this is a Timon who is the precise opposite of the figure adumbrated in his original scheme of panegyric, yet recognisable by us. One is tempted to see in this a lesson for critics. The wordy picture of Timon the Martyr is subverted from below by an invading picture – this time of the real Timon, Timon the Fool. But such an inference is in truth rash. Shakespeare will not make things so easy for us.

It may be said that to analyse the Poet's words in this way is merely a grotesque over-reading of some hastily written lines. If anything which would not occur naturally to the average theatre-goer watching the play counts as over-reading, then the above account certainly stands condemned (though I suspect that a truly exhaustive analysis of spectator response might easily include *some* thought of Icarus, say, even while there would be no leisure to articulate the connections as clearly as Armstrong did). But this kind of moment-by-moment empirical test immediately reveals itself as inadequate when we consider the efficacy (virtually undisputed in drama, wholly undisputed in music) of motifs recurring with modifications at intervals within a single work. It seems clear that a subliminal receptivity to long-term effects, folding past into present, helps us to enjoy long plays and poems. But when all this is said I suspect that Shakespearean drama in a very curious way continues to be coherently explicable *beyond* the natural field of awareness of the average spectator or reader. To pursue such patterns is not at all a matter of free-floating fiction on the part of the critic. Let us suppose a spectator who never thought, hearing these lines, of Icarus. The Armstrong account is then explained to him or her. That spectator might well be capable *at once* of seeing the probability of Armstrong's conjecture and be confident that, while Icarus is relevant, Vulcan, say, is not. It is not the case that just anything will serve. This carries a 'metaphysically realist' implication: that a Shakespearean play is an indefinitely recessive, progressively more and more intelligible object.

I have suggested that the 'Fortune's Hill' speech (I. i. 65–74) is in a manner proleptic of the whole play. It is answered, when the time comes, by a *retrospective* true fiction at V. i. 32, where the Poet says,

> I am thinking what I shall say I have provided for him. It must be a personating of himself; a satire against the softness of prosperity, with a discovery of the infinite flatteries that follow youth and opulency.

But by this stage in the play the allocation of roles, Timon's and the poet's, is plain. Timon says,

> Must thou needs stand for a villain in thine own work?
> Wilt thou whip thine own faults in other men? Do so,
> I have gold for thee.
>
> (V. i. 36–8)

In I. i, there is still room for some uncertainty. The general frame of the speech seems indeed to stress the munificence of Timon and the ingratitude of the rest, but the picture is blurred at certain points. Fortune is enthroned upon her hill. Below, on the flat land, all sorts and conditions labour to improve their lot. One of these is Timon and he it is that Fortune 'with her ivory hand wafts to her' (I. i. 72), whereupon his 'Present grace to present slaves and servants / Translates his rivals', words which are noteworthy for several reasons.

First, 'present grace' ('immediate favour' or 'generosity') is cunningly pivotal. The grace may be exercised by Fortune in her arbitrary selection of Timon (here the thought is almost theological: the generosity of God is for Protestants of this period notably arbitrary). But because the theological implications are here defused in advance by the fact that it is not God but Fortune who chooses Timon, we can allow ourselves to sense a faint resentment at the unfairness of such action on her part. An actor delivering the line about the ivory hand will find it difficult to avoid a sub-acid nuance. The 'present grace', however, may equally be Timon's generosity to those about him. Certainly the effect, whether of Timon's promotion by Fortune or of Timon's own munificence, is to 'translate' or change completely the situation of his rivals. Here again resentment surfaces. For, where we might have expected translation to felicity or to the state of fellow princes, what we actually get is 'to present slaves and servants'. It is instructive to imagine what Timon's reaction to these lines would be, if he were on stage to hear them. Even the word 'rivals' might cause him some distress (we can imagine him saying, 'Not rivals, surely, but friends!'), and as for 'slaves and servants', that surely would shake him profoundly. Because of the curious way in which Shakespeare's mind continually races ahead of itself one can clutch momentarily at the sophisticated idea (later clearly articulated) of a generosity which morally enslaves the recipient, but that can scarcely be deemed to be the *Poet's* intention in speaking as he does at this point in the play. Rather the effect is of imperfectly subdued envy, from a profoundly competitive spirit. This shows again at I. i. 82–5:

> . . . Follow his strides, his lobbies fill with tendance,
> Rain sacrificial whispering in his ear,
> Make sacred even his stirrup, and through him
> Drink the free air.

All the signals here tell us that the devotion shown by Timon's followers is absurd in its servility and that the common air meanwhile is free for all.

But then the Poet pushes on with his narrative of ingratitude. Even here, however, the followers are seen, not as assisted up the hill by Timon, but as labouring after him, presumably by the exertion of their own muscles (I. i. 88). Nevertheless we come at last to the crucial betrayal, as they let Timon slip, 'not one accompanying his declining foot'. Here surely one must accept Rowe's emendation of 'slip down' in place of the Folio's 'sit down' (I. i. 89). 'Sit down' is a common phrase which could easily usurp the consciousness of an inattentive copyist and thus produce a moment of automatic writing. The New Arden editor's attempt to retain the Folio (he suggests, rather oddly, that 'let him sit down' implies 'a sudden push that brings a climber to a full stop') feels merely desperate when one reaches the word 'declining'.

The Painter responds, with the competitive zeal proper to the *Paragone*, saying that his own art can show a thousand moral examples of the world turned upside down. He seems to suppose the Poet has made a like claim for his art, but where in the Poet's speech do we find such topsy-turvydom? Is it implied in Timon's incongruous fall or was it there before in the preposterous devotion of the suitors? The Poet's proleptic fable contrives to be hackneyed and confused at the same time. He has his lines crossed. His ill nature is such that he cannot even produce a straightforwardly generous conventional panegyric. Once more, much of this looks like rough writing. But it is also, with its dexterous exposition of tensions, thoroughly Shakespearean.

We begin to see that it is too easy to say that painting addresses the eye while literature addresses the mind. Drama, in any case, since it is both seen as spectacle and heard as language, occupies an intermediate, or perhaps we could say a double, position. We began by noticing that even printed books (than which nothing can be more 'readerly') can have an impact so immediate as to invite the description 'visual'; after all, we read print, as we watch people, with our eyes. What I have called 'Renaissance alienation' does not always work by abstractions. Resistance to the more ordinary modes of imaginative sympathy can be affected equally well by an unexpected concreteness, by making the reader aware of the physicality of the book in his hand or by stressing the pictorial character of figures on stage which might otherwise be 'read' as richly human psychologies. The fact that the persons in the scene themselves engage in a formal *Paragone* or comparison of visual and literary art strongly suggests, through its technique of studied reduplication, that the effects we found are not accidental but are consciously achieved. The Elizabethans loved to subject properly metaphoric analogies between the arts to an elegant literalism which itself composes as it were an inverse conceit: the 'speaking likeness' becomes the 'Impresa portrait' in which both a human face and some mysterious but authoritative legend figure together within the same frame; *ut pictura poesis*, 'Poetry is as a picture', produced, as the seventeenth century unfolded, increasingly elaborate compositions in which the mere shape made by the type on the page formed an image of the poem's subject. The opening scene of *Timon* does nothing so obvious as this, but belongs nevertheless to the same universe of discourse or imagery. The Poet and the Painter in the opening scene of *Timon* begin to take on a distinctively inhuman concreteness; if they are physical they are so as a signpost is physical. They are not so much talking persons as walking texts, speaking pictures; what else can such beings discuss but the rivalry of signifiers?

· 2 ·

Timon Among the Suitors

Timon enters the play 'addressing himself courteously to every suitor' (another descriptive stage direction). On hearing from a messenger that one Ventidius has been imprisoned for debt, Timon at once agrees to pay what is owed. The messenger in response uses, at I. i. 107, one of the key-words of the play: 'Your lordship ever *binds* him' (my italics). He is saying that Ventidius is now under an obligation to Timon, but we sense that the words are uttered lightly. Even so, Timon seems unable to bear the thought that Ventidius should have even the notional moral advantage of binding himself. He therefore immediately multiplies his original act of generosity many times by pledging indefinite support *after* the debt has been paid. But before we have had time to reflect on any of this an 'Old Athenian' steps forward, braying, perhaps a little too loudly, for Timon's attention. His anxiety is, however, defused and in a manner undercut by Timon's instant courtesy: 'Freely, good father' (I. i. 113). This micro-drama of misplaced energy is again thoroughly Shakespearean. In *As You Like It*, II. vii, Orlando breaks in upon the exiled Duke and his company with drawn sword and is momentarily nonplussed by the civility of his reception.

The old man now thinks himself secure but we learn from the ensuing dialogue that a subtle moral discrepancy between this particular suitor and the lord after all persists.

This is the first application which Timon does not grant at once. The reason is that he is being asked to assist not in an act of generosity but in an act of exclusion. The intelligent spectator will sense the rising difficulty as soon as the old man declares his unswerving allegiance to *thrift* (I. i. 121). 'Thrift', we sense, was not a good word to choose if the object was to persuade Timon. In fact the old man is asking Timon to assist in forbidding his daughter to marry a servant who has sought her hand, since her financial standing implies that she should have a husband in somewhat better circumstances. Timon refuses and instead cuts the Gordian knot by offering, like the King in *All's Well That Ends Well*, II. iii. 173, to build the humble suitor's fortune up to the required level. And of course the old man is delighted to agree. The little dance of asking and giving has been performed a second time, now incorporating an ingenious variation whereby the suit is at first refused but then resolved with a generosity beyond the expectation of the suitor. The completion of the dance leaves Timon, as before, smilingly supreme.

But – also as before – the notion of *binding* is again dropped into our minds, amid the general felicity, to remind us of the nexus of obligation. It occurs simultaneously with the first hint (in 'strain') that Timon's resources are not infinite:

> To build his fortune I will strain a little,
> For 'tis a bond in men.
>
> (I. i. 145–6)

Timon, characteristically, proposes the bond as if it applied in one direction only, requiring simply that *he* should give to everyone else. The old man picks up the idea and, instead of offering a polite expression of reciprocal *moral* obligation, as the Messenger did on behalf of Ventidius before, he reasserts Timon's aphorism, and as he does so actually strengthens the financial reference, though we continue to assume that all this talk enjoys the luxury of a purely figurative mode; again I italicise the crucial words:

Old Ath. Most noble lord,
Pawn me to this your *honour*, she is his.
Timon. My hand to thee; mine *honour* on my *promise*.

The old man does not mean, as some modern readers suppose, 'Engage me also to this honourable commitment', but 'So long as you pledge me your honour in this'. It is left to Lucilius, the newly rich servant, to acknowledge that the gift puts the beneficiary in debt to the giver (I. i. 152–4).

Timon then further accelerates the action by forestalling the Painter's suit. He asks to see the picture before the Painter can so much as pluck his sleeve. From this point, however, the energy begins to fade from the scene, at least for a time, as Timon continues in character, promising to pay lavishly for the picture (though the idea of payment is blurred so that it merges with the idea of a gift-made-freely-in-return – with a general presumption that because the amount is unspecified it is likely to be very much higher than the market price). He turns to the Jeweller and, without prompting, suggests to him a sum higher than the current value of his jewel. When Timon says,

If I should pay you for't as 'tis extoll'd,
It would unclew me quite

(I. i. 170–1)

it may appear, for a moment, that the Jeweller has miscalculated and Timon cannot meet the estimated price. But in fact it is apparent from the Jeweller's baffled reply that Timon is acting out a sort of charade, from pure courtesy: he is politely *pretending* that the jewel is generally agreed to be of immense value. It is likely, though we lack the stage direction, that Timon gives money to the Jeweller at I. i. 175. The Jeweller's nervousness earlier, 'If he will touch the estimate', now appears to have been groundless. By this time the audience has the measure of Timon and is beginning to need something completely different.

This arrives in the person of Apemantus, the antisocial man. Once again the 'dramatic choreography' feels Shakespearean. The movement of the antisocial man within the convivial circle of social beings was done earlier, for example in *As You Like It*, when Jaques enters the pastoral circle, in II. vii. There Duke Senior and his brothers in exile constitute a genuinely loving society, in which the melancholy Jaques must enjoy at best an uncertain status, too sour for friendship, too socially acceptable to function straightforwardly as court fool. In *As You Like It* Shakespeare energises his scene by showing how the naturally affectionate Duke can hardly conceal his hatred for Jaques, whom he sees as a kind of beast (II. vii. 1) opposite to humanity itself. The image used is one of the major, organising analogies of European culture. Behind it lies a seminal passage in Aristotle's *Politics*, dealing with the man who belongs to no *polis*, or 'city' ('community').

> He who is without a polis, by reason of his own nature and not of some accident, is either a poor sort of being, or a being higher than man: he is like the man of whom Homer wrote in denunciation:
>
> 'Clanless and lawless and hearthless is he.'
>
> The man who is such by nature at once plunges into a passion for war; he is in the position of a solitary advanced piece in a game of draughts.
>
> . . . .
>
> The man who is isolated – who is unable to share in the benefits of political association, or has no need to share because he is already self-sufficient – is no part of the polis, and must therefore be either a beast or a god.[7]

In *Timon* the moment of intrusion is managed differently. The society from which Apemantus so vehemently dissociates himself is amicable only in appearance. We have already seen enough to feel some mistrust towards it. Thus the psychological puzzle of sudden hostility which in *As You Like It* is located in the individual, Duke Senior, is here dispersed, though nevertheless implicit in the whole scene. The sociable Timon, who must, like Duke Senior, oppose Apemantus (much as the most indulgent liberal must begin by locking up the Fascist) is shown at first to treat the kill-joy with courteous generosity: 'Good morrow to thee, gentle Apemantus' (I. i. 180). But of course things are not entirely easy. The words 'gentle Apemantus' can hardly be uttered without some effect of irony, in the circumstances. It is possible for the actor playing Timon to underline this, with an arch wink at the others present. But a subtler and more powerful effect is obtained if the line, with all its manifest improbability, is delivered straight. Timon will then look like one acting on some slightly crazed private principle of generosity, schizophrenically blinkered, formalist in his profession of sociability.

The beast imagery, used by Duke Senior of Jaques, here comes first from Apemantus. He replies,

> Till I be gentle, stay thou for thy good morrow,
> Then thou art Timon's dog, and these knaves honest.
> (I. i. 181–2)

The words are manifestly discourteous, but the precise meaning is elusive. The first line is easy enough: 'I am not "gentle", so you'll have to wait a long time before you get any "good morning" from me.' The next line is more difficult. Apemantus is still referring to the future-that-will-never-come, the time when he will be willing to greet Timon. The audience will hear the line confusedly as some sort of jibe, in which Timon is called, insultingly, a dog, and indeed in a way this *is* the meaning-structure. Apemantus is looking forward with relish to a time when Timon shall be reduced to a bestial state. But then the implied conventional insult in 'dog' is turned round: we realise that because Apemantus is against mankind he is deliberately and consciously of the party of the beasts, so that he can say with a degree of sincerity, 'When you are (promoted to the status of) a dog (like me), then and only then can we be friends.'

That the running beast-image in this particular play should be 'dog' is doubtless influenced by a number of extraneous factors. Apemantus is a Cynic and 'Cynic' in Greek means 'doggish'. Pursue this etymology and one comes at last to a mere accident, the fact that the Cynics used to meet at the sign of the White Dog.[8] But the connection with dogs rapidly progresses from the metonymic to the metaphoric. The Cynics *were* dog-like. Diogenes (look at Lyly's *Campaspe*) lived in a barrel as a dog lives in a kennel. Indeed in *Campaspe* the tub is brought on stage at II. ii. 117. Also, most basically of all, dogs are inhuman. The one snag in the picture is that dogs love human beings, but this can be repressed by the artist. It may be said that the ill-fed curs of past ages are likely to have been less affectionate, but what in that case are we to make of the dog Argus who dies happy when his master comes home at last in Homer's *Odyssey* (XVII. 290–7)?

Timon remonstrates, reasonably, 'Why dost thou call them knaves, thou know'st them not?' Apemantus dispatches the objection:

Are they not Athenians?
Tim. Yes.
Apem. Then I repent not.

(I. i. 184–6)

The procedure is at once Euclidian and wildly irrational. Apemantus employs a barely submerged classical syllogism, having the form,

All Athenians are knaves.
X, Y and Z are Athenians.
Therefore X, Y and Z are knaves.

The logic is impeccable, given the premisses, but of

course the major premise, 'All Athenians are knaves', is disputable. Nevertheless, precisely because it is cynical, it will to some extent 'feel realistic'. Presumably because the human race has come to suspect itself of a general tendency to mistake wishes for facts, an opposite presumption develops according to which the pessimistic view is accorded an automatic priority over the optimistic, as if it were inherently more probable. This presumption is culturally strong enough for the present exchange to look like a little victory for Apemantus and a defeat for Timon. Yet at the same time the audience, in some pre-logical, pre-articulate manner, will be profoundly 'with' Timon. Kindred, it might be said, is more than truth. But then intellect can after all come to the aid of kindred, since Apemantus' pessimism really is – is it not? – extravagant.

We have seen little of Apemantus, but enough to make us aware of a lurching, unstable logic in his insults, arising from his rejection not only of human individuals but of their very criteria of approval and disapproval. To put the paradox concisely: 'Dog' is conventionally an insult, but if it is a human convention to use it so, Apemantus must see it as a compliment; but, in that case he is actually in danger of complimenting Timon (the very last thing he wants to do) by calling him 'dog'.

Within a few lines the Painter retorts the insult upon Apemantus, where once again it produces an oddly syncopated syllogism, this time, perhaps, with a curiously childish ring to it:

Pain. Y'are a dog.
Apem. Thy mother's of my generation. What's she,
if I be a dog?

(I. i. 200–2)

Children ascribe an almost magical efficacy to logic or false logic. Consider the following (drawn from life):

First child. What's your favourite animal?
Second child. Cat.

First child.	What's your favourite colour?
Second child.	Blue.
First child.	(triumphantly) That's funny. I haven't seen many blue cats.

At this point the second child ruefully acknowledges defeat. The same tone is present in Apemantus' exchange with the First Lord at I. i. 255–6.

First Lord.	What time o' day is't, Apemantus?
Apem.	Time to be honest.

Compare this time the current 'What's the time?' 'Time you had a watch'. There is perhaps a hint of such playground, magical logic, carried to the point of nightmare, in Macduff's words to Macbeth at v. viii. 15–16:

> Macduff was from his mother's womb
> Untimely ripp'd.

Take away the poetry, take away the tragedy (which is of course to take away a good ninety per cent) and one is left with the echo of a primitive sneer, a verbal trick familiar in every school yard:

> 'Yah! That had you! I wasn't born from a woman, I was born from a corpse!

In the exchange in *Timon* there is little poetry and as yet no tragedy. Instead we have a sort of philosophic paradox whereby high Stoic reasoning is deliberately debased, in an infantile or bestial parody. The form of the syllogism is:

> All those of my generation (i.e. of my manner of coming into the world) are dogs.
> Your mother is of my generation.
> Therefore your mother is a dog (bitch).

Yet here too Apemantus scores a small local victory, through the slashing pessimism of his universal major premise. The Painter has neither the wit nor even the inclination to reply with a *distinguo*. This is not a formal disputation but a sort of fool-baiting. Yet Apemantus is *some* sort of philosopher. That is the way *this* dog bites.

Notice, again, the dynamic logic of Apemantus' reply at I. i. 190:

Tim. Thou art proud, Apemantus.
Apem. Of nothing so much as that I am not like Timon.

This is a brutalist version of something Pope was to do later with great urbanity in the second dialogue of the *Epilogue to the Satires*:

Yes, I am proud; I must be proud to see
Men not afraid of God afraid of me . . .

(207–8)

Apemantus is brutal but he is also elusive. It would clearly not be enough for him simply to deny the charge. This would leave the logical initiative in Timon's hands. He must alter the *terms* of the struggle and this is best done by first assenting and then couching the assent in terms which imply, at a more fundamental level, a dissent far more profound than anything Timon had envisaged when he launched his attack.

So the exchanges continue as the circle closes round Apemantus. At one point the unstable logic of his answers brings him – quite inadvertently – to the brink of blasphemy:

Tim. How lik'st thou this picture, Apemantus?
Apem. The best, for the innocence.
Tim. Wrought he not well that painted it?
Apem. He wrought better that made the painter, and yet he's but a filthy piece of work.

(I. i. 195–9)

Apemantus' last rejoinder is seriously off balance. It begins as a conventional disparagement of human creativity as this appears when set beside the creativity of God; but to praise the Creator is, one might suppose, to praise his creature. As this thought begins to dawn on Apemantus he revolts from his first conception and determines at all costs to preserve his contempt for the Painter (God's creature). Then he is forced to swing back and say that God's workmanship is filthy. Here an ancient theological problem momentarily erupts in a random, uncontrolled fashion. There is in Christianity a traditional escape clause which allows one simultaneously to praise the creator and revile the creature. The mechanism which resolves the difficulty is the Fall of Man. Man was created perfect, but by free will he fell into sin and imperfection. But doggedly to offer this 'solution' in the present case is as absurd as was the earlier suggestion that the Painter might have replied with a *distinguo*. This time, however, it is Apemantus who has lost the thread.

After such exchanges, when Timon asks at I. i. 209, 'How dost thou like this jewel, Apemantus?' it is impossible to sustain any longer the illusion of an ingenuous, utterly straightforward and untainted liberality in Timon. Not that the speech is, conversely, uttered in mere mockery of Apemantus. Timon is really offering and would really have given the jewel and genuine liberality remains the principal motivation. But a *subaudition* of mockery, or even of a kind of sinister temptation, is now inescapable. Christ was in the wilderness when the Devil tempted him with wealth; in Spenser's *Faerie Queene* (II. vii. 2 and 3) Mammon, or 'Wealth', becomes the tempter, and he too lives in a desolate spot. Apemantus is a natural denizen of waste places (for all his haunting of social gatherings), a sort of desert saint without sanctity. Meanwhile Timon is a tempter lacking any clear, authentic vice. Nevertheless, for an instant, the pattern of temptation is there.

Apemantus fights one more syllogistic round before the entry of Alcibiades at I. i. 246, this time with the Poet:

Poet. How now Philosopher?
Apem. Thou liest.

Poet. Art not one?
Apem. Yes.
Poet. Then I lie not. [*First fall to the Poet*]
Apem. Art not a poet?
Poet. Yes.
Apem. Then thou liest. [*Second fall and contest to Apemantus*]

This can be compared (yet again) with an exchange in *As You Like It*:

Audrey. I do not know what 'poetical' is. Is it honest in deed and word? Is it a true thing?
Touchstone. No, truly; for the truest poetry is the most feigning . . .

(III. iii. 17–20)

Both exchanges employ as a major premise, 'All poets lie.' Touchstone goes on to express the earnest hope that Audrey is herself poetical enough to be feigning when she professes honesty – that is, an unwillingness to yield sexually. Apemantus similarly presses on, using the word 'feign' – but here it is Timon who is the object of his reference:

Apem. . . . Look in thy last work, where thou hast feign'd him a worthy fellow.
Poet. That's not feign'd, he is so.

(I. i. 221–3)

Apemantus counters with the principle of reciprocal moral infection which is to govern the play – again using the wrestler's trick of defeating the opponent by a sudden yielding.

Apem. Yes, he is worthy of thee, and to pay thee for thy labour. He that loves to be flattered is worthy o' th' flatterer.

(I. i. 224–6)

He then turns to dispatch the Merchant and again the

note of corrupting reciprocity is struck, though in a different key:

> Traffic's thy god, and thy god confound thee!
> (I. i. 238)

Enter, then, Alcibiades. Apemantus moves to the side of the stage. As he does so his misanthropy shrinks in intensity; his comment is no longer logically subversive but is rather a matter of conventional moralising. The supposedly loving friends are really, he tells us, the inhuman, inhumane ones: 'The strain of man's bred out / Into baboon and monkey' (I. i. 249–50). This clearly implies that there is such a thing as humanity and that Timon's friends fail to measure up to it and are in consequence like beasts, which are properly the inferiors of man. Apemantus here makes no move, say, to identify himself with the baboon and so to subvert the common criteria of judgement. We may sense for a moment that his posture of misanthropy, stoutly maintained as we have seen when he is beset by enemies, is partly a semi-professional hyperbole, a fool's defence, a sort of inverse Uncle Tom-ism. His *difference* from the rest of mankind seems less, when the heat is off.

Alcibiades meanwhile lightens the atmosphere. Shakespeare draws some hints from Plutarch but makes little attempt to evoke the historical Alcibiades, whose disastrous beauty and brilliance at the time of the Peloponnesian War were almost proverbial. Nevertheless he is, discernibly, an attractive figure, with a largeness of movement and gesture, a magnanimity, a generosity and glow of courteous amity which contrasts very sharply indeed with the dourness of Apemantus. Yet (and this is the nature of Shakespearean coherence) within the opening metaphor, offered by Alcibiades with a sort of airy affection, the root idea of parasitism is kept alive by the dramatist; indeed his words put the point in its most basic possible form: 'I feed / Most hungerly upon your sight' (I. i. 251–2). Here we have the biological traffic of eating; below the nexus of economic consumption is the primary consumption of matter itself. Alcibiades means only that he is delighted to see Timon. But words' meaning can be more than speaker's meaning. The idea of men who feed on others is to recur in the play.

But Apemantus does not leave. Instead he stands his ground and is still there when Alcibiades vacates the stage. The grave Latin of the Folio stage direction, *manet Apemantus* ('Apemantus remains'), is oddly expressive. The Cynic skirmishes with two lords and then, at last, takes himself off. The First Lord comments, with philosophic precision, 'He's opposite to humanity' (I. i. 272) and spends no more thought on him. They turn to go into the house where they will be feasted, now talking eagerly, as everyone talks, of Timon. Again the words touch on the fact that gifts may be not simply gifts but also investments, at least where Timon is concerned:

> No meed but he repays
> Seven-fold above itself: no gift to him
> But breeds the giver a return exceeding
> All use of quittance.
>
> (I. i. 276–9)

'Breeds' suggests Elizabethan and Jacobean anxieties about usury (still a morally sensitive area). Shylock said of his gold 'I make it breed', and later in the same scene his great antagonist, Antonio, contrasted this sterile fecundity of metal with human friendship: 'When did friendship take / A breed of barren metal of his friend?' (*The Merchant of Venice*, I. iii. 96 and 133–4). The Second Lord's last phrase, 'use of quittance', is a reference to the customary dates of interest. He is saying, in effect, 'You get a much better rate from Timon.'

· 3 ·

One Playwright or Two?

The second scene of the play begins, as we have it, with a puzzle. Ventidius explains that his father has just died and left him rich, so that he can now repay twice over the money laid out on his behalf by Timon. We have already been shown (I. i. 96–111) how Ventidius was imprisoned for debt and how Timon procured his freedom. The difficulty arises from Ventidius' willingness at this point to repay his debt to Timon. For, later in the play, when Timon is in real need, this same Ventidius refuses to help. Some see this as forming a real inconsistency in the plot.

Two observations, however, can be made in mitigation of the supposed offence. First, Ventidius may know at this point that he can count on Timon's refusal. The fact that he offers to pay twice over does not weaken this presumption. The effect of such extremism would necessarily be a flurry of countervailing courtesies from Timon. Ventidius, we notice, puts up no fight when Timon refuses repayment. Instead he beams and cries, 'A noble spirit!' (I. ii. 14). All of this could easily be communicated by a reasonably accomplished actor, who, if he wished to labour the point, might move ponderously to offer the money and register mild relief when Timon refused his offer. This would get a laugh and actors like to get laughs.

Secondly, Ventidius' later refusal may well be influenced by the *smell of disaster* which by this time hangs round the figure of Timon. As Lucius says, 'He that's once denied will hardly speed' III. ii. 63).

Nevertheless the sequence is not altogether comfortable. One's sense that more work needs to be done by the dramatist grows stronger if one consults the Folio. It is not just that the playwright is unclear about his character's motivation; at the same time he seems less than certain of his name. In I. i, when Timon undertakes to relieve Ventidius, the name is spelled just so: 'Ventidius'. In I. ii, the scene now before us, when Ventidius attempts to repay his debt to Timon, he is called in the Folio 'Ventigius'. In II. ii, when Timon instructs his steward to apply for help to Ventidius, the name is now given as 'Ventiddius', while in III. iii, at the point where we hear of his refusal to assist, the name appears as 'Ventidgius'. We have, then, four versions of the name: 'Ventidius', 'Ventiddius', 'Ventigius' and 'Ventidgius'. Some infer from this not just that *Timon of Athens* is unfinished, but that we have before us a plain case of multiple authorship. It is not necessary, of course, to infer four authors, one for each version, since the first pair, 'Ventidius' and 'Ventiddius', can readily be seen as alternative spellings of the same name and the same is true of the second pair, though it remains odd that one man – author or compositor – should spell the same name in two different ways; I would guess that it is about as unusual as for a twentieth-century person to write the date according to different conventions on successive cheques (a rare thing but not unknown, for I know that I do it myself); one thing we know about Shakespeare is that he spelled his *own* name in more than one way (see the six accepted signatures, reproduced on page 1,696 of the Riverside Shakespeare).

The New Arden editor points out that names are spelled differently in the second quarto of *Hamlet* by a single compositor setting directly from Shakespeare's foul papers.[9] More pertinently still, the compositor of *Timon* managed to write 'Lucilius' and 'Lucillius' within four lines.[10] We need to remember that such variation, as I have implied, feels odder to us in the twentieth century because English spelling as a whole has become fixed, as it was not in an age when a compositor could 'spell long or short' to justify his page (that is, to achieve a pleasingly rectangular block of print on the page).

At this point, however, it is proper to recall that the very presence of *Timon of Athens* in the Folio is attended with various marks of dubiety. It appears that William Jaggard, the publisher of the First Folio, ran into difficulties when the time came to insert *Troilus and Cressida*. It seems that the first thought was to place this play among the Tragedies, but suddenly there was a change of plan and *Troilus and Cressida* was placed between the Histories and the Tragedies. At this point, it appears, *Timon of Athens* was brought in to fill the position which *Troilus and Cressida* would have occupied according to the original design (between *Romeo and Juliet* and *Julius Caesar*).

Charles Knight in *The Pictorial Shakespeare* of 1838 seems to have started the fashion of disintegrating the play among several authors.[11] This view was still going strong in 1910 as is shown by E. H. Wright's monograph, *The Authorship of Timon of Athens*.[12] The reaction against disintegration had however already begun. W. Wendlandt in the *Shakespeare Jahrbuch*, 23 (1888)[13] argued that the text of *Timon* derives not from a collaboration of two authors but from an unfinished draft by Shakespeare. F. S. Boas in *Shakespeare and his Predecessors* (1896) trod carefully, admitting the likelihood of collaboration but insisting that it is now virtually impossible to separate the non-Shakespearean work from the Shakespearean.[14] Then in 1908 (the Red Letter edition), E. K. Chambers threw his weight behind the Wendlandt view[15] and later reaffirmed this opinion in his *William Shakespeare* of 1930.[16] Una Ellis-Fermor's article, '*Timon of Athens*: an unfinished play', *Review of English Studies*, 18 (1942) 270–83, is widely regarded as having finally routed the disintegrators.

Yet the theory of collaboration will not lie down. In 1920 Thomas Middleton's name had entered the discussion. Middleton was an active figure in the theatrical world of London from the early 1600s to the late 1620s. Today he is remembered chiefly for *The Changeling* (written with the help of William Rowley) and for *Women Beware Women*, but his range is wider than these plays alone would suggest. He was a great professional, writing by turns masques for important city occasions, comedies and tragedies. He is more intelligently interested than most of his contemporaries in social difference and money. He seems to have enjoyed working in collaboration with others. William Wells, in a flinty little note,[17] argued that Middleton was responsible for I. ii and III. i–vi in the existing text and that Middleton had written a play on the Timon story in his early comic period; this play was then partially revised by Shakespeare. Three years later, in the same journal, H. Dugdale-Sykes went still further.[18] Though both of these attempts to enlist Middleton were disparaged by Samuel Schoenbaum in his *Middleton's Tragedies*,[19] the case for Middleton's participation continues to persuade some of the most competent authorities. MacDonald P. Jackson's *Studies in Attribution: Middleton and Shakespeare* (Salzburg: Universität Salzburg, 1979) argues carefully, from patterns of linguistic usage, that Wells was essentially correct in ascribing I. ii and III to Middleton, though he adds, 'Nevertheless, even within I. ii and III there are some passages which I should be happier attributing to Shakespeare than to Middleton.'[20] Lastly, I understand that, at the time of writing, Roger Holdsworth's work on stage directions is tending to confirm the Wells–Jackson analysis.

It is a field in which certainty is elusive. Even if we assume, for the sake of argument, that Middleton wrote I. ii and III and that Shakespeare chose not to interfere, while this accords perfectly with the two basic versions of Ventidus' name ('Ventigius' or 'Ventidgius' now becomes the Middletonian version), we have made no progress at all with the problem of motive and consistency with which we began; or perhaps one should say (since, if my earlier argument is right, there may in fact be no serious inconsistency to explain) the *theory of collaboration* does not help us resolve the 'problem' of Ventidius' motivation. The supposed inconsistency is between I. ii. where Ventidius behaves generously, and III. iii, where he behaves ungenerously, but both of these scenes are given to Middleton.

It remains true that the severest disintegrator cannot *confidently* banish Shakespeare from a single line or phrase. Jacobean collaborators can scarcely be supposed to have worked in separate cells. They would have talked to each other, and either writer would have gone to work with the other's words running in his head.

Let us take an example. After Ventidius has been dealt with Apemantus steps forward and observes that it grieves him 'to see so many dip their meat in one man's blood' (I. ii. 41). This is an image of power which seems to exist in a very curious way at a point of intersection between Middleton's genius and Shakespeare's. There is more than a hint of anthropophagy in the line and cannibalistic imagery is characteristic of Middleton.[21] But we have already seen in the thoroughly Shakespearean opening scene how the idea of feeding on a person was (with great delicacy on the author's part and entire courtesy on Alcibiades', who was speaking at the time) applied to Timon himself, at I. i. 251–2. Also in I. i, Apemantus says, 'I eat not lords' (204). The language of Apemantus in I. ii (the scene commonly given to Middleton) then renders the thought explicit in precisely the right manner. At the same time this, the more sanguinary version of the idea ('dip their meat in one man's blood'), has a certain relationship with the moment in *Julius Caesar* when Brutus tells his fellow conspirators to stoop and wash their hands in the blood of the newly slain Caesar (III. i. 106). There is no reference to *drinking* blood in the *Julius*

Caesar passage, but a more shadowy connection with *Timon* can be traced. Brutus is performing an oddly perverse ritual, washing away the pollution of blood with blood (he saw the murder of Caesar as a *sacrifice*, II. i. 166), and in *Timon*, as we shall see, the idea of the feast as the ritual of amity will grow stronger as the play proceeds, the whole being subjected to a kind of bloody parody. Moreover the (cannibalistic) current English expression 'blood-thirsty' is readily applicable to Brutus' words. Meanwhile, in the *Julius Caesar* episode, Mark Antony, the hostile observer, is moving into the circle of those bound by their crime and their exalted ideas. In the dynamics of the scene, though not of course in character and motivation, he corresponds to Apemantus in *Timon* I. ii. And of course the idea of cannibalism, though absent from the *Julius Caesar* passage, occurs elsewhere in Shakespeare. In *Hamlet* the King asks, 'Where's Polonius?', and his nephew tells him, 'At supper':

> *King.* At supper? Where?
> *Hamlet.* Not where he eats, but where a' is eaten; a certain
> Convocation of politic worms are e'en at him.
>
> (I. iii. 17–21)

It is like an Apemantus'-eye-view of Timon. In *Troilus and Cressida*, a play having a general affinity to *Timon of Athens* (the more likely perhaps if both were, as E. A. J. Honigmann thought, written for coterie audiences at the Inns of Court[22]) we have 'He that is proud eats up himself' at II. iii. 154. In *Coriolanus*, another Plutarchian play and likely to be close in date of composition to *Timon* (1607–8), we have the First Citizen's 'If the wars eat us not up, they will; and there's all the love they bear us' (I. i. 85–6), where love and charity are turned into a kind of cannibalism. Later in the same play the Second Servant marvels that Coriolanus is now being feasted by Aufidius, his former enemy, and speaks of Coriolanus' own very different treatment of Aufidius at Corioles: 'And had he been cannibally given he might have boil'd and eaten him too' (IV. v. 188–9). This time the process runs in reverse, perverse anthropophagy miraculously converted to convivial feasting. Lastly, in what is perhaps the most Shakespearean speech in *Timon* the protagonist says, 'You must eat men' (IV. iii. 428). In *Timon* I. ii. 75–9 the thought is given a further twist in an exchange between Timon and Alcibiades:

> *Tim.* You had rather be at a breakfast of enemies than a dinner of friends.
>
> *Alcib.* So they were bleeding new, my lord, there's no meat like 'em; I could wish my best friend at such a feast.

This could well be Middleton but, again, it is oddly reminiscent of other things in Shakespeare. The word 'breakfast' and the context of praise accorded to the hearty man of war evokes Prince Hal's description of Hotspur in the First Part of *Henry IV*, 'He that kills me some six or seven dozen of Scots at a breakfast' (II. iv. 102–3). Cross Hotspur with the blood-obsessed Coriolanus and we come very close to the Alcibiades of *Timon*. Breakfast and friendship go together again at *Henry V*, II. i. 11, 'I will bestow a breakfast to make you friends.' Indeed it is the last clause of Alcibiades' speech which comes closest to forging an imaginative link between the (otherwise creakingly separate) Alcibiades motif and the story proper in this play. For who is Alcibiades' best friend? Who is *everyone's* best friend? The answer is Timon, who sits indeed at just such a feast as Alcibiades wishes for him, with one difference: he is to prove not the eater but the eaten. I do not claim, then, that Apemantus' speech on dipping meat in Timon's blood is not characteristic of Middleton. I only add that it is as thoroughly Shakespearean a thought as one could well find.

Act III of *Timon* begins with the brilliant succession of episodes in which the various persons approached by the now desperate Timon find reasons for turning him down. In modern editions this covers III, scenes i to iv. The Folio text gives no scene-divisions at all for this play; this is probably the result of some editorial accident, but the feeling of fluidity it produces nevertheless seems apposite. The successive figures of refusal compose, as it were, a single dance. I have called it brilliant, but (now we are perhaps pressed harder) is it Shakespearean brilliance? It is here that MacDonald Jackson, the best of the disintegrators, scores his most elegant triumph:

> In his excellent little book, *Shakespeare and the Confines of Art* (London), 1968, Philip Edwards remarks that if *Timon* had missed publication in the First Folio 'we should not have known . . . of Shakespeare's power to write satirical merchant comedy in a style which only Middleton can equal. The scenes in which, one after another, Timon's beneficiaries find excuses for not helping him in his need (the first three scenes of Act III) are brilliant, and have no parallel elsewhere in Shakespeare' (p. 134). One is reluctant to set any limit to Shakespeare's powers as a dramatist, but is it not likely that scenes in 'a style which only Middleton can equal', with 'no parallel elsewhere in Shakespeare', and as thoroughly Middletonian in their pattern as they are Shakespearean, are in fact Middleton's, not Shakespeare's?[23]

This is neat, but perhaps too neat. The Middletonian flavour of III. i–iii is strong (the verbal parallels with *Michaelmas Term* II. i and II. iii are especially striking[24]). But the pacing of the scene and the verbal energy can feel Shakespearean (I do not know whether 'can feel' requires an apology: I offer none). Meanwhile the general dynamics of *Michaelmas Term* II. iii are very different. There Quomodo, the usuring shopkeeper, is hoping to get Easy, a wild young man, into his clutches and for this purpose incites his man, Shortyard, to assume a false identity, to befriend Easy and so draw him into borrowing from

Quomodo. All the excitement turns on whether Easy will or will not be caught by the strategies.

At the same time, while there may no parallel to the movement of the *Timon* scenes in earlier Shakespearean comedy, in Shakespearean histories we find, repeatedly, scenes in which relief is withheld and loyalties betrayed. In the First Part of *Henry VI* the heroic Talbot finds himself in extreme need; York and Somerset temporise, each blaming the other (York says at IV. iii. 9–14 that he could have helped Talbot had not Somerset let him down and at IV. iv. 1–9 Somerset charges York with the failure of the relief force). The swift cutting of the scenes (again not marked in the Folio, as with *Timon*) is not unlike the rapid movement from creditor to creditor in *Timon*, as Emrys Jones has pointed out.[25]

In *Richard II* it is the King who is let down and this time the initial draining away of confidence which leads to the betrayal is expressed in explicitly financial terms. The gossip about Richard could be transferred, almost without change, to Timon:

Willoughby.	The [King's] grown bankrout, like a broken man.
Northumberland.	Reproach and dissolution hangeth over him.
Ross.	He hath not money for these Irish wars.

(II. i. 257–9)

In III. ii, first Salisbury and then Scroop bring news that help is not forthcoming. Scroops says,

Sweet love, I see, changing his property,
Turns to the sourest and most deadly hate.

(III. ii. 135–6)

These words will serve as a sententious summary of *Timon*, with just a hint, perhaps, of a Timonian equivocation on the word 'property' (from 'character uniquely appropriate' to the idea of ownership: 'property' in the sense which is dominant today). Compare the way Timon, at I. ii. 100, affirms that it is the defining character or property of a human being to confer benefits and, as he speaks, begins to shift the meaning, away from logic, towards ownership.

Jackson himself allows that Shakespeare probably revised Middleton's work[26] and, as we saw, confessed that even in Act 3 there are things which look more Shakespearean than Middletonian. Once more we should admit that we do not know. There is no reason why criticism should be paralysed by such an admission. Some person or persons made a play, and the play itself is in our hands.

The arguments for regarding *Timon of Athens* as a collaboration are too strong to be ignored. But, if there was such a collaboration, it appears to have been of the kind which, while it might produce blunders at the technical level – spelling, continuity and the like – nevertheless passed images and ideas from hand to hand with great tenderness. I have already suggested that this must be the case with the idea of cannibalism. Later we shall see how, in scenes given to Middleton, the far more important ideas of grace and eucharist are developed in close accord with what is likely to have been an originally Shakespearean conception. Once again, we surmise, the 'collaborators' must have talked to each other, and that talk is likely to have been so intense that it is really idle to say of certain cardinal images that they are finally the exclusive property of either dramatist. *Timon of Athens* is one play not two, superficially disfigured by technical inconsistencies but conceptually and imaginatively coherent.

· 4 ·

The Suitors Press Harder

Apemantus is, for a declaredly antisocial man, oddly given to turning up at gatherings. Although we may say (and have said) that his philosophy makes him a natural inhabitant of the wilderness we perceive that in fact he is no more a hermit than he is a natural participant. We need a third term, and perhaps the best is 'watcher'. Though he will take no part he is clearly deeply interested in his fellow creatures. To say of X that he is keen on football is ambiguous. It may mean that he likes to play or that (like the manservant in *Being There*) he 'likes to watch'. Apemantus himself says at I. ii. 34, 'I come to observe.' It is thus clear that Apemantus *spectator haud particeps* is keen on society in the second sense; he is indeed almost a connoisseur.

Because Apemantus is frozen in the posture of critic-spectator he is in a manner timeless. Every Shakespearean fool is a player within the play, performing for the persons of the drama as they perform for us. Apemantus is an *auditor* within the play; it is not so much that he is further *in*, more deeply embedded in the fiction, as that he is further *out*, almost one of us. Nevertheless, because he is not causally locked into the life-plot of the other characters he can be used by them as fools are used in other plays. Timon seems to sense this special timelessness; he jibes at the fixed humour of Apemantus at I. ii. 26–9. *'Ira furor brevis est*', he says, borrowing from Horace ('Anger is a brief madness'), 'But yond man is very angry'. In Apemantus the state of furious indignation is continuous, or even strangely static. One intuits an authorial meaning beyond the speaker's meaning. We have already noted that this is a play of strangely schematic identities (for which the Renaissance word is 'humours'). In this scene, one who is beginning to descend on Fortune's Wheel addresses one whose misanthropy is constant – almost house-trained.

Apemantus pronounces his anti-grace (of which more later). Once more, as in I. i and afterwards at I. ii. 82, the First Lord, confident of his security, implores Timon to make *some use* of his friends – to draw on their assistance (here too the word *use* is not entirely cut off from its connection with 'usury'). Timon becomes agitated. His own declared conception of friendship is liberality and he must not deny the status of friend-in-his-own-right to the First Lord; that is, he must allow *him* to be liberal. But it is evident that some dark, driving necessity of his inner nature will not let him take his turn as beneficiary in the financial dance of amity. Timon answers, in rather confused and confusing prose, that simply to be a friend is to confer a benefit and that he hopes to have many such benefits in the future. He in effect metaphorises the First Lord's material conception of service, so that the base metal is sublimed out, but then, as soon as he is safe from any possibility of receiving financial benefit, Timon allows himself to develop the original, material notion, as a free-floating, courteous optative:

> Why, I have often wish'd myself poorer that I might come nearer to you. We are born to do benefits; and what better or properer can we call our own than the riches of our friends? O what a precious comfort 'tis to have so many like brothers commanding one another's fortunes.
>
> (I. ii. 98–103)

It is a moment of great intensity. The language is working with superadded energy, as we may see in the force of 'properer'; it means, 'more fitting', but includes a hint of ownership ('propriety'/'property'/'proprietorial') so that a minor paradox of private ownership suddenly exploded through amicable exchange is generated. Timon is strongly moved; tears well up in his eyes (I. ii. 104). There is a sort of mild hysteria in the air; Timon's tears are infectious:

> *Second Lord.* Joy had the like conception in our eyes.
> And at that instant like a babe sprung up. (I. ii. 107–8)

Schoolteachers used at one time to describe certain children as 'unhealthily imaginative'. The Second Lord's language remains eagerly polite but, for all that, his imagination (or the playwright's) seems to be running away with him. If Tilley is right there is a reference, *within* the idea of rising joy as a newly conceived infant, to the lovers' practice of looking into one another's eyes so that each sees himself or herself reflected in miniature. The image is here too fugitive to be developed, yet, potentially at least, it is an extraordinarily apt emblem of separate self-identity preserved even in the most intimate expression of reciprocity or union. Perhaps Apemantus picks this up when he says harshly, 'I laugh to think that babe a bastard' (I. ii. 109).

The most important thing of all about this speech is still unsaid. Timon's words are a classic expression of irony, running at full Sophoclean strength. This strange flurry of intense yet displaced (hypothetical) lachrymosity will, when Timon's real, desperate need becomes obvious, seem merely appropriate. Then indeed there will be matter for tears. The poet has played a present oblique emotion against a possible – or even imminent – future with great skill. Whoever did this knew how to write plays.

The same cannot be said of the Masque of Amazons

which follows. We cannot know what the dance was like: the text conveys nothing. The myth of the Amazons is as rich as most myths are but there is no sign in the present passage that this wealth of potential signification is used in any way. Here we have a situation in which the interpretative critic is driven almost to despair. The most ingenious response is probably that of John M. Wallace[27] who suggests that a masque not of Amazons but of Graces was originally intended. Everything then falls into place; the Graces are the Senecan Graces from Book I of *De Beneficiis*, Giving, Receiving and Returning, and are subsequently transformed by Shakespeare into bizarre prayers, Graces-before-eating. One longs to believe it.

But Cupid and his ladies are soon gone. Timon and his guests proceed to dinner. The second note of disquiet is sounded by the Steward when Timon calls for his jewel-case (I. ii. 154). Earlier Timon has hinted that he is aware of his impending difficulties, with the words, 'To build his fortune will I *strain a little*' (I. i. 146, my italics). From here on the presumption seems rather to be that Timon is *oblivious* of his situation. Thus the Steward has the greatest difficulty in getting him to take appropriate action. Given a text as manifestly faulty as *Timon*, one certainly cannot rule out the possibility of inconsistency at this point: in I. i a Timon who knows something at least of his plight and in I. ii a Timon who knows nothing. But, equally, it remains entirely possible that what the more mechanical reader takes to be inconsistency is in truth a fine psychological subtlety. A Timon who half-knows and suppresses his half-knowledge is not *fundamentally* implausible.

Then the presents begin to arrive. First, as it is announced that certain nobles have arrived, Timon says, 'They are fairly welcome' (I. ii. 172). A servant tells Timon that Lucius has presented him with four horses and he answers, 'I shall accept them fairly. Let the presents be worthily entertained' (I. ii. 182–3). Another servant brings an invitation to go hunting from Lucullus and notice of a present of four greyhounds. Timon says, 'I'll hunt with him; and let them be received, / Not without fair reward' (I. ii. 188–9). 'Fair', 'fairly' and then 'fair' again: these are slippery terms, but a certain progression can nevertheless be detected in Timon's replies.

Beginning from the root sense 'beautifully', *fairly* can take on meanings like 'auspiciously', 'honorably' and 'kindly'. The last is the most appropriate for Timon's first reply, but we need to be aware that the word *kindly* is itself subject to a curious etymological identity-crisis in courtesy exchanges; if I say, 'I thank you kindly', whose is the kindness, yours or mine? The case is similar with the 'fairness' of the welcome offered in Timon's first answer. In the second and third replies, however, the sense 'equitably' begins to invade. The reason is not far to seek. The First Servant brought news of a social call only. The Second and Third Servants bring news of gifts. This, so far from relieving the hard-pressed Timon of anxiety, makes him slightly more anxious, more strenuous in his liberality than he was before. In his second reply one senses the sub-text, 'It is only fair that I should accept', or else 'I shall accept in a manner you will find equitable'. For Timon, as we have seen, gifts are not just gifts; they are occasions to be matched and over-matched by counter-giving. The semantic shift in *fairly* shows this with great economy. That such a shift from 'kindly' to 'equitably' really is happening is implied by the word 'worthily' in the second reply and is clinched by 'reward' in the third.

What is happening in this scene is that certain common tropes of civility, such as 'I'd be honoured if you would accept this trifle' or 'You'd be doing me a good turn if you'd let me help you', normally innocent or even socially healing in their effect, begin as it were to be taken too seriously and to generate an uncontrolled regress of moral anxiety. Taken in this way such forms can instigate a competitive, ever-accelerating transference to and fro of the burden of obligation. The benefactor implies by his courteous assumption of the role of beneficiary (even as he presents his gift) that, had he not offered this special absolution in advance, the recipient would naturally be in debt to him. It is obvious to any ordinarily intelligent person that such polite expressions of reverse obligation are artificial or merely formal. If, however, they are over-emphasised in practice they re-emphasise the reality of the obligation incurred by the recipient. To one whose social nerves are as raw as Timon's, as soon as a giver goes through the absolving preamble, it is clear that the situation is irremediably infected with the idea of reciprocal obligation. In ordinary social intercourse none of this matters. To Timon it matters very much indeed. For him the only release is by giving in return, always more than he has been given.

Meanwhile, as the Steward explains in his soliloquy, all these victories in the courtesy-contest of liberality must be paid for, with ordinary money:

> His promises fly so beyond his state,
> That what he speaks is all in debt; he owes for ev'ry word:
> He is so kind that he now pays interest for't.
>
> (I. ii. 195–7)

The scene draws to a close with Timon divided between his keen interest in Alcibiades, as a sort of anti-type to himself, and a distracting confusion of confessed (notional) obligations. By this time the audience knows that all the while Timon really owes and is owed much. Through all this Timon is fascinated by Alcibiades' strangely pre-economic method of livelihood. We remember that Aristotle said of the unsocial, unpolitical man that he loved war (*Politics*, 1253a). Alcibiades is not yet clearly marked as antisocial. Unlike Apemantus he has, and retains, all the social graces. Only gradually in the play will it become apparent that he, rather than Apemantus, is to be the true ally in misanthropy. Alcibiades is interested not in friendship but in fighting, not in the lending of money but in the letting of blood. Timon, the apostle of convivial friendship, says almost enviously:

> . . . for all thy living
> Is 'mongst the dead.
>
> (I. ii. 222–3)

After the disorienting subtleties of high manners, with their interplay of real with unreal, meaning with unmeaning, the Second Act begins more simply. We have seen the beneficiaries of Timon's munificence. Now we see an actual creditor. The decent Senator who stands before us is owed money by Timon and has been owed that money for a long time. Deadlines have been missed and the Senator's own credit has been damaged (II. i. 22–3). We become aware that there are those whom Timon continually loads with gifts and there are others to whom he will not give a penny, although – or, should we say, because? – in the second case he really owes them what they ask for. This creates a minor difficulty at the level of plot. The Senator himself, in the middle of his account of the difficulty of getting money out of Timon, stumbles on the fact that there is one very simple way to activate Timon's pathological munificence:

> If I want gold, steal but a beggar's dog
> And give it Timon – why, the dog coins gold . . .
>
> (II. i. 5–6)

It might seem, then, that the Senator's course is simple. Let him tear up his bonds and proofs of loan and instead present Timon with – say – a canary. This, quite automatically, would provoke a gift from Timon of much greater value. It is because we are in an oddly schematic play that such solutions, at once elegant and insane, occur.

One might have expected that the technical, artistic difficulty might have been eased by making the creditors socially distinct from the friends; the former, for example, could have been hated, professional money-lenders. The author of *The Merchant of Venice* must have been aware that this solution lay ready to hand. But in *Timon* he does not clearly avail himself of it. The Folio stage direction calls the creditor of II. i 'Senator' and this at the very least implies a person of high social standing. Moreover, the Senator's words at II. i. 23–5 suggest the embarrassed friend rather than the professional usurer:

> I love and honour him,
> But must not break my back to heal his finger.
> Immediate are my needs . . .

In the following scene, however, the Fool asks the servants of Isidore and Varro (also creditors) whether they are 'usurers' men' and the servants agree that they are (II. ii. 99–100). Yet this is scarcely enough to cancel or clarify the impression made by the Senator in II. i. The Folio *dramatis personae* calls Lucius 'a flatt'ring lord' but the same list refers confusedly to his man (calling *him* 'Lucius') as 'servant to a usurer'. III. iv, as we shall see, is a veritable merry-go-round of usurers, creditors, friends and beneficiaries on which the audience is likely to become thoroughly confused. In this very confusion, however, the author may be mirroring existing social conditions more accurately than is commonly realised. To obtain the severe separation of usurers and gentlemen so much needed for a crisp dramatic point, the playwright must set his drama in Venice where, notoriously, the most basic usurers of the system were segregated in a real ghetto. It is true that Italy was also famous for the fact that gentlemen there did not feel the automatic contempt for trade which was found in England. Thus, Fynes Moryson, writing in 1617, observes:

> The Gentlemen disdain trafficke, thinking it to abase Gentry; but in *Italy*, with graver counsell, the very Princes disdain not to be Merchants by the great, and hardly leave retailing commodity to men of inferiour sort. And by this course they preserve the dignity and patrimony of their progenitors.[28]

In Venice, however, this very openness was in a paradoxical manner made easier by the presence of a separate, despised class available to do the most obviously dirty work. Antonio, after all, though he despises Shylock, is unashamedly a merchant.

No such clear image is provided of the economic arrangements in the virtually ahistorical setting of *Timon of Athens*. So instead we have a kind of fidelity to confusion: Lawrence Stone has suggested that the money-lenders at the end of the sixteenth century ranged from rich merchants to lawyers, ambassadors and noblemen. It is almost as if money-lending was in practice more acceptable socially than trade. A moment ago I used the image of a merry-go-round. Stone uses the same image:

> The system was a gigantic merry-go-round, with the great moneyed men of London paying each other off every six months or so. When in 1593 the Earl of Shrewsbury was trying to borrow £5,000 from Sir Horatio Palavicino to clear off a debt to Thomas Sutton, the former remarked that 'Mr Sutton was his neighbour and yt had been his happe to be his paie-master manie tymes'.[29]

II. ii opens with the Steward, as ever, wringing his hands at Timon's prodigality. He offers a moral formula, which will be re-evoked later:

> Never mind
> Was to be so unwise, to be so kind.
>
> (II. ii. 5–6)

That is, Timon really is immensely generous and the more distressing aspects of his behaviour are due to folly. The explanation almost satisfies, but not quite. The note of desperation in the Steward's next words, 'He will not hear', suggests a state of mind in Timon beyond ordinary unwisdom.

Enter then the servants of more creditors, Caphis (the Senator's man) and those of Isidore and Varro. These address one another by the names of their masters. It may be that this was a known idiom in Shakespeare's day, but it still seems highly likely to have caused mild confusion in the theatre, where the audience is trained to rely on vocatives as straightforward indicators of identity. The Folio editors, as appears from the *dramatis personae*, seem themselves to have been misled.

Then Timon emerges and we see exactly what happens when he is confronted not with gentlemanly liberality but with a creditor who needs to be paid. He refers the importunate servants to his Steward, suggests that they call again the next day and in general succeeds in making them look awkward and ill bred. Presumably in real life the great men, as often as not, bullied the usurers. There is hardly a hint of this in the drama of the period, but perhaps we glimpse it in a single line from Middleton's *A Mad World, My Masters*: the disguised servant, speaking of Lord Owemuch, says that he was 'free o' the mercers, and there's none of 'em all dare cross him'.[30] Timon is helped here by English class feeling which can work in an anti-mercantile (anti-capitalist) manner. In Whetstone's *Mirrour for Magistrates of Cities* (London, 1584), leaf 4, all the animus is reserved for the merchants and usurers, and none for the spendthrift gentlemen who squander all.[31] A splendidly clear though late specimen is offered by Sheridan's *The School for Scandal* (1777), where the lovable upper-class scapegrace Charles Surface is warned by his friend Rowley that he should not lavish money on a poor relation when his debts are now pressing. Charles quotes a proverb which (for once!) works on behalf of the creditor, but then instantly subverts it:

Charles S. Be just before you're generous – Why, so I would if I could; but Justice is an old lame hobbling beldame, and I can't get her to keep pace with Generosity, for the soul of me.

Rowley.	Yet, Charles, believe me, one hour's reflection –
Charles S.	Ay, ay, it's all very true; but hark'ee, Rowley, while I have, by Heaven, I'll give; so damn your economy![32]

Sheridan clearly feels that he can count on an automatic gust of approval from the audience. In *Timon* this same sentiment of approval is exploited, but the matter is complicated by two factors. First, the objects of Timon's generosity, unlike Charles Surface's poor relation, are undeserving. Secondly, as we have seen, the social status of the creditors is bewilderingly entangled with that of the friends, though in the present scene that particular difficulty is eased by the fact that the bills are presented by servants. In general the effect is far more open-textured, the sentiments more jagged, than in the Sheridan scene.

Throughout this episode of gentlemanly, arrogant evasion, Alcibiades stands at the elbow of Timon like a *kōphon prosōpon*, or 'dumb mask', in a Greek tragedy. He seems to be there as an extreme anti-type, now, to the creditors' servant. Alcibiades, we guess, is one who is equally likely to enter your house with a gift or a sword, but will never present anyone with a bill (hence the shock, later in the play, when he stoops from his aristocratic height to ask a favour from his city).

But at last Alcibiades and the Lords withdraw, and Timon turns to his Steward to address the problem. That he should do so in the form of an implied, gentle rebuke to the Steward for not informing him earlier is an excellent touch. Still better is the fact that the Steward in reply does not even bother to defend himself but at once seizes the opportunity and simply calms the creditors' servants by fixing a later appointment, in a manner wholly different from Timon's a few moments before. It is quite impossible to construe Timon's indignation as authentic, noble surprise. We have been given a stream of indications that repeated attempts have been made to apprise him of the facts. Later in the same scene Timon and the Steward return, and pick their way over the same ground more carefully. Timon reiterates his amazement (II. ii. 128–9) and the Steward overwhelms Timon's flimsy complaint with a vivid account of his repeated efforts to communicate the real state of affairs. Timon in this exchange seems not so much disingenuous as mildly schizophrenic; it is as if part of his mind can express a perfectly sincere amazement (an amazement which must in the circumstances be perceived as absurd) while another, saner part of his mind must always have known the truth. The crucial moment of acknowledgement comes in four bleak monosyllables at II. ii. 158: 'You tell me true.' The words represent, very precisely, not an act of learning but of recognition.

Apemantus and the Fool enter as Timon and the Steward leave, at II. ii. 50. Again we notice a surprising degree of affability, indeed of positive helpfulness beneath the misanthropic surface of Apemantus. When the Page comes in with a letter whose address he cannot read, Apemantus, after the obligatory preliminary growling, reads it to him. What is more the Page is obviously not in the least afraid of Apemantus (your friendly neighbourhood misanthrope) but assumes from the beginning that he will help. The 'flyting' which follows is almost spiritless, but certain key words, *dog*, *grace*, *usurer*, are kept alive by mere mentioning (II. ii. 89–90, 91, 99). Then, as Timon re-enters, Apemantus calls the Fool with a sudden urgency:

> Come with me, fool, come.
>
> (II. ii. 124)

There follows one of those speeches of strange, isolated beauty, which seem in Shakespeare to come from nowhere:

> *Fool.* I do not always follow lover, elder brother and woman; sometime the philosopher.
>
> (II. ii. 125–6)

The words are strong, even before they are understood.

Presumably the point is that all the relations discarded, whether of love or family, are interested. The philosopher alone gives mere truth. All humanity, even perhaps all love, resides with the relations here, for the moment, rejected. There is a barely discernible hiatus in the comedy, and then the Fool skips out, behind the grotesque Apemantus.

The scene closes with Timon and the Steward together recognising that extreme action is called for, and with Timon's dispatching his servants to borrow from his friends. Timon, beaten down by the Steward's words into a brief, numb submission, lifts his head again as he lights on the saving formula, 'Unwisely, not ignobly have I given' (II. ii. 178). This, as we saw, was pre-echoed by the Steward's 'Never mind / Was to be so unwise to be so kind', at II. ii. 5–6. Timon's line is reminiscent of Othello's 'One that lov'd not wisely but too well' (*Othello*, V. ii. 344). Timon's speech, like Othello's, is the apologia of a defeated man. In both there is a curious feeling that the speaker is still not able fully to perceive or understand the truth he acknowledges. H. J. Oliver in the New Arden note observes that Timon's judgement on himself is finer than that given by many commentators. At the same time, however, it is manifestly insufficient. 'Unwisdom' such as Timon's is not a simple explanatory feature; it in its turn holds inner complexities and tensions which invite a more strenuous effort on our part to understand. The point is clearly underlined by the word 'conscience' immediately following: 'Canst thou the conscience lack, / To think I shall lack friends?' (II. ii. 179–80). 'Conscience' is here used in the old, morally neutral sense and means 'knowledge' or 'awareness'. The inadvertent irony is complete, for it is Timon not the Steward who lacks awareness.

The Steward explains that he has already applied to the Senate on Timon's behalf. Timon's response is to shut down half his mind and to take refuge in hearty optimism: the Senators are old, sluggish and therefore have nothing to offer but ingratitude (the *King Lear* word, 'ingratitude', is strong despite the generally struthious context). Ventidius, Timon argues, is different; he will help. The words which close the Act are the Steward's and they are enigmatic. It is perhaps worth noticing that Timon's words which prompt the Steward's mysterious reflection are, in their strict grammatical form, not a simple assertion of confidence but a negative injunction *not* to be aware, *not* to think.

> *Tim.* Ne'er speak or think
> That Timon's fortunes 'mong his friends can sink.
> *Stew.* I would I could not think it.
> That thought is bounty's foe;
> Being free itself, it thinks all others so.
> (II. ii. 234–8)

The Steward probably means, 'I wish I could control my thought in the way you ask. But thought is free, and that means that thought (intelligence) is the natural enemy of munificence like yours; thought will pursue its own track, regardless of duty and friendship, and so naturally it takes the cynical view that others would suppress.' That is, he picks up the idiom used lightly by Timon as a way of saying 'I can't possibly founder with so many friends to support' and insists on understanding him at a more literal level. It will be seen that in this interpretation I differ from the New Arden editor. He, with some hesitation, takes the speech from 'That thought', to mean, 'That belief (that one's friends will not desert) is the enemy to a truly generous person – *because* it means that he gives his money away to those who will not reciprocate'. The New Arden editor's note takes no account of 'free'; moreover, it takes 'that thought' to be the thought that friends will *not* desert, that is, the optimistic thought expressed by Timon's entire sentence. But Timon, *within* his sentence, used the word 'think' and in the circumstances the Steward's use of 'thought' will unavoidably be heard as taking up that word and pursuing it. The thought alluded to – and forbidden – by Timon is that friends *will* desert.

5

Timon Slighted by his Former Friends

The escalating sequence of reasons given by the friends for refusing to help Timon is managed with great art. Lucullus in III. i says, in effect, 'I warned him that he was behaving imprudently; it's a bad time to lend money; here, have three Solidares – and you never saw me.' In III. ii, Lucius says, in effect, 'How very unfortunate; I would have been delighted to help, but I just happen to be short of money at the moment.' Lucius (a nice touch, this) says that he is shocked and saddened by the behaviour of Lucullus, using as he does so the curious idiom, 'I am asham'd on't' (III. ii. 17). Formally the words seem to express personal guilt, but that is not of course what Lucius means. The moral shame is not his – he is sure of this – but Lucullus'. We can compare the Fool's observation in *King Lear* that we – not Tom o'Bedlam himself – would all have been *shamed*, had not Tom kept one blanket to cover his nakedness (III. iv. 65–6). It appears that shame can be socially diffused as mere embarrassment. Meanwhile, however, the audience is vividly aware that Lucius has reason to be ashamed in the central meaning of the word. In III. iii Sempronius at first wonders why Timon has not applied elsewhere, but, on learning that he has done just that, instantly takes full advantage of his position in the sequence; he affirms that he is insulted by Timon's not having turned to him in the first place.

Readers, unlike spectators in a theatre, can refer back at this point – to II. ii. 191–7. There they will find (if they had forgotten) that the dispatch of servants was as nearly simultaneous as it could well be: 'You to Lord Lucius; to Lord Lucullus you (I hunted with his honour today); You, to Sempronius.'

The Third Servant's comment on Sempronius is oddly difficult. The audience has just watched what may be described as either a monstrous display of hypocrisy or a sequence of consummate satirical art, depending on whether the description applies inside or outside the fiction (what the person in the story does as against what the playwright or the play does). The Servant, although firmly placed as a character within the fiction, seems by his first word to place himself outside it. 'Excellent', he observes (III. iii. 29). The appreciation expressed is no doubt ironic, yet our awareness that this is so does nothing to destroy our momentary sense of an *aesthetic* response from the Servant. In the logical limbo of the 'aside' or in the kind of soliloquy which is also in some degree an address to the audience, such intermediate effects are possible. The Servant goes on, 'Your Lordship's a goodly villain.' The use of *villain* to mean 'evil character in a work of fiction' (as in 'villain of the piece') seems not to occur clearly before the nineteenth century, but uses like the present one prepare the way for it. The difficult part of the speech follows:

> The devil knew not what he did when he made man politic; he crossed himself by't: and I cannot think but in the end the villainies of man will set him clear. How fairly this Lord strives to appear foul! Takes virtuous copies to be wicked, like those that under hot ardent zeal would set whole realms on fire: of such a nature is his politic love.
>
> (III. iii. 29–36)

The New Arden editor points out that 'him' in 'will set him clear' could refer to man or to Satan; if the former, then the whole phrase means, 'will release him from his debt'; if the latter, it probably means, 'will make him (Satan) appear innocent by comparison'. Malone believed the second explanation and is followed by J. C. Maxwell in the New Cambridge edition. But of the two meanings the former is linguistically the more natural. Even today we speak of 'being cleared of debt'. The context strengthens this presumption. The word 'crossed' just before strongly suggests, as the New Arden editor rightly says, a financial metaphor of some sort, hovering in the writer's mind. The word 'clear' occurs again at III. iv. 75, immediately following the phrase 'pay his debts'. Indeed, the larger context of the entire play, with its continual reference to bonds, debts and obligations strengthens the presumption still further. If we venture beyond the play and later in time, we may think of the famous reference to a recovered innocence in *The Winter's Tale*: '. . . the imposition clear'd, / Hereditary ours' (I. ii. 74–5).

The sense, however, remains puzzling, and it is not surprising that commentators should hesitate. Why should the devil be *frustrated* when man pays his debt to Satan; that, surely, is exactly what the devil wants? The answer must be that it is *not* what the devil wants. The devil actually prefers that man should remain for ever his creditor. This is certainly not set out clearly enough for audience or reader to pick it up with any security, yet it is profoundly in tune with the running logic of *Timon*: the nexus is all; those who give with the most complete unselfishness actually expect something in return, namely gratitude, and, when the time of real need comes, may further expect that such gratitude will express itself in the form of hard cash. Those who hate mankind, meanwhile, find themselves linked with mankind, in the converse sociability of a shared, and enjoyed, hatred. Language is nexus, and as long as we use language we are involved with one another. These involvements may smell of Heaven or Hell.

According to such a conception of things it becomes

easy to see that the devil will defer the payment of debts, even to himself, as long as he can. Indeed, even within orthodox theology the question arises, was Satan pleased or frustrated when Christ discharged the human debt with his own life? There seems to be little doubt that the fundamental conception behind these words of the Third Servant is theological, but it is as if different theologies are entwined or confused. The devil may have gnashed his teeth when Christ snatched away his victim, but there the debt was cleared by a great art of self-sacrificing love, not villainy. In stories like that of Dr Faustus, one pays one's debt to the devil by surrendering one's soul to perpetual evil, which seems a little closer to the idea of clearing the debt by villainy. Meanwhile, although Christ redeemed the world by love the mechanism of redemption entailed that, in the mysterious phrase of Scripture, Christ should 'be sin for us' (2 *Corinthians* 5: 21). Augustine in chapter 51 of his *Enchiridion* raises the question whether there is textual authority for the idea that Christ sinned and decides that there is not. Luther, however, in his 1535 *Lectures on Galatians* affirmed that Christ on the cross was accursed of God and guilty of all sins.[33] In such moments of extreme Protestantism we seem to have crossed back again to the idea of a debt discharged by wickedness.

In the present passage it is probably impossible to determine a firm underlying framework, but it may be that the very confusion of good with evil in the discharge of obligation, which here frustrates commentary, reflects in a vague manner the basic impulse of the play. The writing seems almost wilfully obscure. 'How fairly this Lord strives to appear foul' almost looks like a case of transposition ('fairly' for 'foully' and 'foul' for 'fair'), at least as long as we take 'strive to appear' in its most natural (purposive) sense. But Sempronius is not, like Jonathan Swift, an inverse hypocrite, who delights 'in seeming worse than he was'.[34] Presumably we must take 'to' as consecutive rather than purposive, so that the phrase means, 'strive with so much strenuous gracefulness, only to be, manifestly, evil'. An actor could convey this meaning by emphasising the word 'strives' and pausing after it. But the speech looks half-finished, with its uncertain modulation from prose to verse (is 'of such a nature is his politic love' the last sentence in the prose section or the first line of verse?) The general sense of the speech is in the right area and is indeed concerned with relations of great subtlety, but one can scarcely maintain that this represents high art, deliberate rich ambiguity or the like. It looks much more like a case of half-digested thought.

The same sense of failure to clinch what might otherwise have been some kind of moral paradox or epigram pervades the following scene (III. iv) in which the servants of the creditors discuss their masters' position. We have already noticed what may well be a deliberate decision on the dramatist's part not to draw a firm social distinction between low professional usurers (to be ignored) and friends (to be treated liberally). The etymology of *liberal* itself suggests that liberality is proper to free men (*liberi*) and has nothing to do with slaves. One may think also, going still further back, of A. W. H. Adkins's brilliant observation that in early Greek society a *kakos*, 'a bad/base man', is one on whom we can inflict *kaka*, 'bad things', with impunity.[35] This class-divided morality could have been made to yield both irony and dramatic tension, but in the present scene the matter is managed in an uncertain fashion.

Take the following exchange:

Titus. Your Lord sends now for money?
Hortensius. Most true, he does
Tit. And he wears jewels now of Timon's gift,
For which I wait for money.
Hort. It is against my heart.
Lucius's Servant. Mark how strange it

shows,
Timon in this should pay more than he owes:
And e'en as if your lord should wear rich jewels,
And send for money for 'em.
(III. iv. 19–25)

Hortensius' master apparently is both a creditor and a beneficiary of Timon's liberality. He is sending for money but, at the same time, he wears a jewel Timon gave him. To buy this jewel Timon has borrowed from the master of Titus. The comment of Lucius' servant is quite sharp. Hortensius' master, he says, is sending for money which he has already received in the form of the jewel.

One looks for a certain comedic structure at this point: something like: not only do Timon's *friends* show ingratitude in his moment of need; his *creditors* show a like ingratitude, since they themselves have in the past profited by his munificence. But the idea is not forcefully pursued. Lucius and the master of Hortensius have received gifts from Timon. All, according to the Steward at III. iv. 50, have been dined by Timon. But it remains untidily possible that some of them are simply creditors and therefore that they are genuinely ill used by Timon, in so far as they have afforded him money from their own stocks and this money has not been repaid. Indeed, one can see that the alternative picture, which gives us simply a pack of creditors who are all, originally, beneficiaries, presents certain difficulties. If Timon's liberality had been throughout confined to them, the entire operation now sought by him would be a recycling of his own wealth, with no input from outside. The entire problem would appear to be capable of a mathematical solution: if the original gifts were valued and the value entered against the debt, in the (improbable) event of a perfect match in each case, the bankruptcy of Timon would simply vanish into thin air. Of course the creditors will not write off debts against earlier gifts in this way, but one senses that the dramatist wants Timon's situation to be a good deal blacker than this in any case. He wants him to be plunged deep in genuinely unpayable debts, debts which would remain unpayable even if the gifts were accepted as currency.

Nevertheless the idea of merging the beneficiaries with the creditors is, inherently, a promising one. What is needed is a clear episode in which the creditors take an ostentatiously gentlemanly line on the absolute distinction between gifts (accepted graciously and then placed on one side) and debts (to be pursued relentlessly).

It remains odd that the satiric comedy continues to work more strongly against the creditors than against the debtor. Even when Timon is reduced to hiding in his house, afraid to come out (III. IV. 37), and his Steward to muffling his head in a cloak (III. IV. 41) they have not become the figures of fun a summary of the scene would suggest. Neither Timon nor his Steward ever begin to take on the comic/pitiable status of Micawber, say, evading his creditors in *David Copperfield*. The classical antecedents of the Timon story tend, as Lee saw in 1916, to blacken the character of the hero.[36] *Timon of Athens* was probably written at a time when Shakespeare was closely engaged, on several different fronts, with such classical sources as Plutarch's *Lives*. *Coriolanus* is likely to have been written at roughly the same time as, or near in time to, *Timon*. The stage would seem to be set for a humiliation of the spendthrift and the Cynic, along the lines of Roman comedy. Yet, as we have seen, the current of satiric indignation flows, for much of the time, in a contrary direction in *Timon*. It is not that the play is obtusely uncritical of its main character. Rather it is as if there is consistently available to the writer a factor of automatic sympathy for Timon, a factor on which he can count.

6

Digression
Some Jacobean Attitudes

Certainly feeling against usurers was strong in 1607. In 1934 J. W. Draper mounted a massively documented demonstration of this.[37] The essence of his case is that in Shakespeare's presentation of Timon a traditional literary conception which is largely hostile or satirical is invaded and transformed by a (to us) bizarre emotional sympathy, this sympathy springing not from literary sources, but, in an oddly direct manner, from current social reality. The stock Elizabethan Timon is a cynical hater of God and man. Barckley,[38] de l'Espine,[39] Rowlands[40] and Brathwaite[41] all show him in this light. Nor is any sympathy for Timon to be discerned in the similarly stock allusions in Lyly, Mulcaster, Greene, Nashe, Lodge and Dekker.[42] Meanwhile, however, in the real world the English aristocracy were passing through an economic crisis. The old military powers of the nobility were being eroded by the rise of the professional soldier.[43] Roman Catholic families in particular were subjected to punitive taxation. Rapidly climbing interest rates enriched the merchant but impoverished the lord. Dekker inveighed against the flow of gold from America.[44] 'Usury', says Draper, 'seemed the cause that enriched the new families and destroyed the old.'[45] He further notes that even Bacon (the 'modern man'), while he approved of interest upon loans, regretted the fact that high rates were ruining the county families;[46] Philip Caesar describes the effect of usury as 'honest men beggared . . . hospitality hindered, charity extinguished'.[47]

Draper, it may be said, strains too hard. The Timonian figures in the literary tradition are in fact regarded not with simple hostility but with a complex mixture of derision and appreciative admiration. It is true that these figures are not far removed from Fools, but even Fools are ambiguous, inviting both sympathy and self-dissociation. In Lyly's *Campaspe* there is a notable episode, taken from Plutarch, played between the great King Alexander and the Cynic Diogenes (the latter a likely source for Shakespeare's Timon).[48] Alexander upbraids Diogenes for his refusal to attend at the Palace and asks him – with a strange gentleness – whether he owes no reverence to kings. Diogenes answers that they are no gods and when Alexander quibbles, saying they are 'gods of the earth', Diogenes bleakly agrees, but alters the sense as he does so: 'Yea, Gods of earth' (II. ii. 130). Alexander is left asking, almost wistfully, 'How should one learn to be content?' to which Diogenes replies, with measured authority, 'unlearn to covet' (II. ii. 148). One might have expected so radical a rejection of hierarchy to be instantly crushed, but that is not what happens. Alexander finds himself strangely paralysed by the words of the Cynic. In part, no doubt, we are to understand that Diogenes' freedom is a kind of Fool's licence (there is no danger in an allowed philosopher) yet he is more than Fool and Alexander's response is very different from, say, that of Olivia in *Twelfth Night*: 'What think you of the fool, Malvolio? doth he not mend?' (I. v. 74). Alexander says, '*Hephestion*, were I not *Alexander*, I wolde wish to be *Diogenes*' (II. ii. 148–9). The response of Hephestion, the judicious onlooker, is not simple but mixed: 'He is dogged, but discrete; I cannot tel how sharpe, with a kind of streteness; ful of wit, yet too wayward' (II. ii. 150–1).

In like manner Shakespeare's one reference to Timon before the play of that name is tantalisingly elusive in its tone. In *Love's Labour's Lost* the witty Berowne, having listened, in hiding, to the lovesick language of men who only a little before had dedicated themselves to learning and high-minded seclusion, steps forth, as he puts it himself, 'to whip hypocrisy' (IV. iii. 144). His speech of (really quite good-humoured) castigation includes these lines:

> O, what a scene of fool'ry have I seen,
> Of sighs, of groans, of sorrow, and of teen!
> O me, with what strict patience have I sat,
> To see a king transformed to a gnat!
> To see great Hercules whipping a gig,
> And profound Solomon to tune a jig,
> And Nestor play at push-pin with the boys,
> And critic Timon laugh at idle toys!
>
> (IV. iii. 161–8)

Draper included this reference in his catalogue of anti-Timonian passages. Perhaps he ought to have hesitated. Certainly the passage is a specimen of mock-heroic – mock-heroic of a distinctively Renaissance kind; the venerable Nestor playing with the little boys is a brief gesture of irreverence towards the Master of Troy, of a kind which seems always to have gone down well with the young wits at the Inns of Court. It is an early version of a mode which will, in time, be elaborated in *Troilus and Cressida*. But it is important to remember that the mockery in mock-heroic can work in either direction. The ancients may be themselves dishonoured by low comparisons, or else the moderns may be exposed to ridicule by being set against a lost, genuine nobility. Here the main force of the speech is of the latter kind. The presumption is not that Timon's misanthropy was mad or vicious but rather that a Timon who ceased to be sternly judicial would be a Timon who had betrayed his proper office.

The word 'critic' is especially interesting. It is at this date an exceedingly rare word, with a strong smell of academe, of Greek etymological origins. Berowne is unlikely to be using it in an adverse sense, as meaning 'caviller', say, since earlier in the play he had applied the word to himself: 'I, forsooth, in love! / That have been love's whip . . . a critic!' (III. i. 174–6). The logic of the earlier reference mirrors that of the later: as long as Berowne despised frivolity, like the transformed Timon, he was admirable. Such must be the speaker's meaning and such, therefore, the lexical sense of the word. But the larger context of the comedy tends as it unfolds to endorse a contrary, deeper wisdom founded in love, and therefore perhaps to cast a new, less friendly light on the unsocial, unloving posture of the critic. The Epistle to the Reader, prefixed to Dekker's *News from Hell*, which post-dates *Love's Labour's Lost* but probably ante-dates *Timon* by one year, contains the words, 'Take heed of *Critics*: they bite',[49] which is, if we are precise, not an example of *critic* used with an adverse *sense* but rather an explicitly hostile remark about critics – a quite different thing. Bacon, that thermometer of innovation, uses the word in a wholly favourable sense in *The Advauncement of Learning* (1609), I. vii. 21. Philemon Holland, on the other hand, implies a certain dubiety in the role of critic when he says, 'I am forced even against my will to be after a sort *criticus* . . . but to find out a truth.'[50]

The literary tradition, then, is not one of unmitigated hostility. On the other side, the social feeling of the time may not have been as uniformly sympathetic to the fate of the distressed nobility as Draper suggests. He himself notices that Coke, Bacon and a special Star Chamber decree of 1614 condemned the noble practice of duelling, observing that this is exactly the kind of thing Alcibiades runs up against when he pleads for his friend.[51] Yet there must have been a body of, so to speak, anti-Alcibiadean feeling to have produced the legislation. The tableau of the Gentleman Ruined by Usurers, displayed over and over again in the writings of the period,[52] has not been understood until it is seen in tense relationship with a rising Puritan emphasis on the virtue of thrift.

Lawrence Stone is clear that the phenomenon is essentially dialectical: the arrogance of the Elizabethan aristocracy is symptomatic of insecurity; the attempt to revive and indeed exaggerate the old open-handed ways served only to accelerate the downfall.[53] Nor should one suppose that within the aristocratic ideology the cult of liberality always obliterated all sense of obligation towards creditors. John Smyth of Nibley was proud that he could claim that in twenty generations the family of Berkeley had never left a debt unpaid, while the less happy Earl of Leicester in his will of 1587 expressed his shame and grief at the losses he had caused those creditors whom he had not been able to pay.[54] *Timon of Athens* explores dramatically the ways in which liberality can turn sour; first and most practically, by plunging the giver in debt, secondly and more subtly, by inextricably entwining the notions of generosity and obligation, gratuitousness and gratitude. When Robert Morgan built Mapperton Hall in the 1540s and 1550s he had inscribed in the hall:

> What they spent, that they lent;
> What they gave, that they have;
> What they left, that they lost.

Morgan is echoing a line put into the mouth of the soon-to-be ruined Mark Antony – so Seneca tells us – by the now forgotten poet Rabirius:

> *Hoc habeo, quodcumque dedi.*
> Whatever I have given, this I possess.[55]

The special Stoic–Elizabethan tone of these verses, rejoicing as it were in the very unreality of what they assert, is instructive. The nexus of gratitude and obligation, with its queer symmetrical resemblance to the ordinary requirements of fair financial exchange, is evoked as a kind of mixture of aristocratic wish fulfilment and accomplished fact. It is a joke of course, but is full of pride. It is a miniature obverse of *Timon of Athens*, undoing, by a stroke of wit, all the sequence of evils set forth in the play. Nor are these isolated examples. Polonius, as everyone knows, advised his son to steer clear of the entire business: 'Neither a borrower nor a lender be' (*Hamlet*, I. iii. 75). It may be said that Polonius is hardly an exemplary character, but there is no serious question but that these words of his would have been construed by the audience as good, prudent advice.

Nevertheless the general effect of Lawrence Stone's work is to corroborate the picture presented by Draper. Even if Stone may be thought in some respects to have overplayed his hand, making a national crisis out of something which was really a London (Court) phenomenon, this makes little difference to the literary question before us. Stone points out that some two-thirds of the peerage found themselves in severe financial difficulties in the last fifteen years of the age of Elizabeth.[56] The practice of usury was regarded with an almost universal horror. This, Stone affirms, 'was not mere lip-service to an outdated mediaeval tradition. It was deeply and passionately felt by a society in which indebtedness was both an almost unavoidable necessity and a terrible social scourge.'[57] If one thing is clear it is that these were *nervous* times, economically. After 1590 price fluctuations became vertiginous.[58] We are dealing with a society, and hence with a literature, which has discovered the instability of money.

Where does this leave our understanding of Shakespeare's *Timon*? The modern reader who proceeds too swiftly to see the play as a straight attack on neurotically exaggerated munificence is in error. The dogged exhumer of pamphlets on the evils of usury who concludes therefrom that the playwright's sympathy for Timon is unalloyed is, likewise, wrong. The method of the play is to incorporate a degree of moral sympathy for the protagonist normally forbidden in satire, and then, having moistened many an eye in the audience, to drive relentlessly on with the less comfortable implications of Timonian liberality. Of course the distinction between folly and baseness – 'unwisely not ignobly'

(II. ii. 178) – is no panacea; for it is not as if folly were exempt from moral criticism. But nothing in the bizarre sequence of events ever cancels or retrospectively removes the sympathy accorded to Timon's bizarre generosity. There is a kind of converse sentimentality which is satisfied only by a severe separation of sheep and goats; by this rule there are contemptible persons who should be satirised and admirable persons who should be applauded. That is seldom Shakespeare's way. What, he says, of the good man whose very goodness runs awry and produces evil effects?

Timon's generosity is indeed so intense as to suggest (as we have seen) an obscure competitive anxiety which is itself the opposite of real love; it is clear that one who gives so unremittingly must do so with his eyes shut tight, so to speak, against the human reality surrounding him, and such a person can have no friends. The best chance of friendship Timon has is with trusted servants, precisely because he need not be for ever loading them with gifts. We have noticed that Shakespeare is careful in this play to give Timon no wife, no child. It is time to link this denaturing of the protagonist to the denatured character of usury itself. Aristotle was a great biologist before he was a philosopher. It is often observed that the teleological habit of his mind, his continual emphasis on growth and purpose, arises from his intense investigation of natural process. When Aristotle writes about usury, he is struck most of all by the monstrousness of a kind of growth which has no foundation in nature:

> The natural form, therefore, of the art of acquisition is always, and in all cases, acquisition from fruits and animals. That art, as we have said, has two forms: one which is connected with retail trade, and another which is connected with management of the household. Of these two forms, the latter is necessary and laudable; the former is a method of exchange which is justly censured, because the gain in which it results is not

> naturally made but is made at the expense of other men. The trade of the petty usurer is hated most, and with most reason: it makes a profit from currency itself, instead of making it from the process which currency was meant to serve.
>
> Currency came into existence merely as a means of exchange; usury tries to make it increase. This is the reason why usury is called by the word we commonly use [the word *tokos* which in Greek also means 'breed' or 'offspring']; for as the offspring resembles its parent, so the interest bred by money is like the principle which breeds it, and it may be called 'currency the son of currency'. Hence we can understand why, of all modes of acquisition, usury is the most unnatural.[59]

This sense of unnaturalness never dies in the Jacobean period. Antonio in *The Merchant of Venice* plays upon it with his scornful question, 'When did friendship take / A breed for barren metal of his friend?' (I. iii. 133–4). Thus Timon has no family, save in the old sense of 'household'. The word *economy* comes from a Greek root, present in the passage cited from Aristotle, which means 'management of the household'.

Yet, when all this is said, the giving was great. If we lose the sense, quite inescapable in theatrical presentation, that this is a play about one who loved or tried to love his fellows, by giving away enormous amounts of money, and substitute a uniform, unmixed contempt for the protagonist, the play is dramatically impoverished.

· 7 ·

Timon Furibundus

Towards the end of III. iv, the creditors close in on Timon's door. Lucius says:

> Methinks he should the sooner pay his debts,
> And find a clear way to the gods.
>
> (III. iv. 74–5)

In this derisive speech the word 'clear' moves from its financial sense ('clear of debt') to a more elusive meaning, having affinities with 'clear conscience' and even, more simply, 'clear sky' so that it seems for a moment to hold out the possibility of another, better world. Even as the creditors move in there is shouting within and Timon emerges, as the stage direction says, 'in a rage': *Timon furens*. The direction is oddly stilted but this is in accord with the alienated character of the play. We have moved from the stereotypical *Paragone* of the opening to a still more schematic reversal of character. Timon's giving is replaced, with deliberate abruptness, by Timon raging. The thing works theatrically because the anxieties of the audience have been fomented to the point at which an explosion of some sort is desired. The closing net of creditors supplies the place of a psychologically articulated transition in Timon. But this does not mean that the dramatist is aiming at plausibility by mere default of attention. He wishes us to feel the very inhumanity of the change.

The timing of the speeches is marvellously controlled. Timon bursts from his house and his anguish breaks out in richly figurative language, but the creditors merely watch and press in upon him, as the assassins of Caesar closed round him at the death.

> *Tim.* The place which I have feasted, does it now
> Like all mankind, show me an iron heart?
>
> (III. iv. 81–2)

In the dialogue which follows the language of Timon histrionically enacts a fiction in which he is murdered; the language of the creditors reasserts the cold reality that what they want is money not blood. The sequence, which becomes more and more powerful as it develops, begins from an almost absurd equivocation by Timon on the word 'bills', which can mean either 'accounts' or 'weapons'.

> *Philotus.* All our bills.
> *Timon.* [Perhaps spreading his arms, as if on a cross] Knock me down with 'em: cleave me to the girdle.
> *Lucius' Servant.* [Embarrassed by Timon's language] Alas, my lord –
> *Tim.* Cut my heart in sums.
> *Titus.* Mine, fifty talents.
> *Tim.* Tell out my blood.
>
> (III. iv. 88–93)

There is a hint here of the exchanges between Richard II, with his taste for hyperbole, and the factual Bolingbroke. In either play there is a secondary realism within the seeming unrealism of the words coming from the less stable party: Bolingbroke really was deposing Richard; the creditors really are taking Timon's life away. Money is very like blood. But, in so far as rational and irrational elements in Timon's speech are separable, one must say that the irrational are given greater space, more room to strut in. It is as if Timon knows that poetry is magic and will create a space – a respite – for the man possessed by it:

> Weave a circle round him thrice . . .

Thus Timon's display which may be a mixture of real and feigned passion has achieved the desired result. The creditors back away and leave him. As they depart, Timon is suddenly calm again, perhaps because it is only now that he conceives his plan of action. The barometric needle swings again from Gloomy to Fair. Timon will give another feast. The Steward shakes his head but to no avail. Timon is confident that he will be able, when the time comes, to provide.

III. v is a curious, imperfectly assimilated scene in which Alcibiades pleads on behalf of a friend – not on Timon's behalf, notice, but for another friend, whom we never meet in the rest of the play. At the level of ordinary plotting this scene is almost superfluous. Thematically, however, one senses an obscure but powerful kinship with the main plot. Both are concerned with a sudden blow struck against older, aristocratic values. I have urged that a kind of admiration should coexist with our disapproval of Timon's behaviour. It would seem that a similar argument must be mounted here, in favour of Alcibiades, against an almost insuperable twentieth-century hostility. Yet in the case of Alcibiades it is hard to avoid the inference that the aristocratic ideology is now, so to speak, at the very limit of its tenure: that his case sounds strained and is meant to sound strained. His language does not contain even the secondary, reflected warmth of the term 'ingratitude' appropriated for Timon from the richer world of *King Lear*, though it could easily have figured in the diatribe against the Senate at III. v. 112–15.

Alcibiades, we learn, has a friend who has killed a man. His reputation was impugned so he struck back, fatally. Alcibiades outlines the whole affair, gentleman to gentlemen, with breezy confidence. I am aware as I write this that others have reacted very differently to this speech, finding, for example, 'human heartedness'[60] where I find an unacceptable (and revealing) lightness of manner. Alcibiades seems to be unaware of any need to specify the nature of the insult to his friend, to explain the degree of provocation. He says that his friend acted 'in hot blood' (III. v. 11) but the hot blood was, so to speak, entirely normal; this seems to be the meaning of 'with such sober and unnoted passion' at III. v. 21. Setting this action aside, he is, says Alcibiades, a splendid fellow.

But how on earth can we set this action aside? It is the very point at issue. Moreover the speech is tricked out with certain airs and graces of decorative pseudo-argument which are little short of offensive: Alcibiades' friend showed no fear as he killed his man, so that the virtue of courage may be said to have made up for the vice of murder(!). However often we remind ourselves of sympathy felt by Jacobeans for duelling noblemen, the First Senator's reproving response sounds, quite simply, just and moderate:

> You undergo too strict a paradox,
> Striving to make an ugly deed look fair.
>
> (III. v. 24–5)

The words which follow, on 'valour misbegot', are philosophically magisterial; they are not unlike Hector's sober rejection of Troilus' excited plea for honourable slaughter in *Troilus and Cressida*, II. ii. 168–87. The speech is eloquent – and much more persuasive than Alcibiades' – but it too is oddly lacking in moral warmth. Alcibiades could have been given a Christian answer. Instead we have antique Stoicism curiously combined with an insinuation that Alcibiades and his kind are out of date. The Stoicism shows plainly in

> He's truly valiant that can wisely suffer
> The worst that man can breathe.
>
> (III. v. 31–2)

The suggestion of superannuated values comes when the

Senator says that false valour properly belongs to a time when sects and factions were newly born (III. v. 30). We are close to the antinomy in *Coriolanus* (a play similarly unenriched by Christian warmth) between the violence of Coriolanus, the man of war, and the co-operative values suddenly held in high esteem by cities at peace with their neighbours.

Alcibiades perceives at once that a civic (civilised) response has simply ruled out his fundamentally martial assumptions:

> My lords then, under favour, pardon me,
> If I speak like a captain . . .
>
> (III. v. 42–3)

Again *Coriolanus* is relevant and so is Plutarch, drawn on for that play and this. Plutarch in his *Life of Coriolanus* comments on the consuming interest taken by the Romans in *andreiotēs*, *virtus*, 'virility', or 'manliness'. Shakespeare quite clearly picked up this hint and deployed it against the other, contrary suggestion, also in Plutarch, that Coriolanus was to an almost disquieting extent devoted to his mother. Here, in *Timon of Athens*, Alcibiades, presumably destitute of serious arguments, equivocates on the Stoic ideal of 'bearing', and replaces the usual meaning 'endurance' with the sense 'giving birth'; from this silly pun he infers that the Senator's view is just a way of turning men into women.

The equivocation is not wholly frivolous of course. It is sustained from below by the real antagonism, already noted, between martial (virile) values and civic (intersexual?) values. Like Coriolanus, Alcibiades has one material argument – produced at last in III. v. 60–3 – that his friend has *earned* special treatment by his warlike deeds. This is a powerful argument, but in so far as there is a loose presumption that a civil, mercantile, co-operative society tends to follow rather than to precede a society which lives by war and rapine, it tends implicitly to reinforce the Senator's earlier suggestion that society moves on, so that Alcibiades and his kind are less highly valued than formerly. Yet even here the movement of sympathy is not finally stilled; some will be moved now by a special pathos in Alcibiades' situation rather than by an obvious intrinsic rightness in the arguments he advances. The Second Senator counters Alcibiades' reference to exploits on the field of battle, very precisely, with a reference to the friend's presumably very similar behaviour in the streets of the city: 'He's a sworn rioter' (III. v. 69).

The affinities with *Coriolanus* are here so strong as to suggest that Shakespeare wrote this dialogue or, at the very best (since we do find 'has' for 'hath' in the scene, commonly accounted a sign of Middleton's presence), that Shakespeare carefully and fully revised a Middletonian draft.

The real reason, I suppose, why critics talk of 'human-heartedness' with reference to Alcibiades springs from the character's own contention that his friend's behaviour was above all *human*. Here the pattern of his rhetoric is like that of Berowne in *Love's Labour's Lost*, written some twelve years earlier. Berowne argued similarly that human passion is forgivable because it is inextricably involved with our moral nature. He ends with the words,

> And who can sever love from charity?
>
> (IV. iii. 362)

Alcibiades' words are similar, even in cadence:

> To be in anger is impiety;
> But who is man that is not angry?
>
> (III. v. 57–8)

To be sure, the yawning difference between Berowne and Alcibiades is in the end more instructive than the formal resemblance. For where Berowne was saying 'Love is natural to human beings' Alcibiades is very nearly saying the precise opposite. We are in the presence of a misanthropy so complete that it does not even know that it is misanthropy.

The plea failed. But Alcibiades was unable to understand that it had failed. He pushed on with the Coriolanian argument that his friend's service in war had earned him indulgence. We must grant, of course, that *Timon of Athens* does not present, as *Coriolanus* does, a developed contrast between the virtues which are valued in time of war and those which are valued in time of peace. We sense, even before the Second Senator counters, that Alcibiades' argument from service is no longer secure in its effect. Again we have a gentlemanly equivocation in

His service done
At Lacedaemon and Byzantium
Were a sufficient briber for his life.

(III. v. 60–2)

The word 'briber' is offered by Alcibiades as a mock-apologetic metaphor, on the assumption that the auditor will understand that what is really at issue is not illicit persuasion but straightforward desert. But there is some danger that the word will be taken almost literally. We may compare the very free use in current English of the phrase 'moral blackmail'. Once again, as so often in this play, an image drawn from the world of financial relations is so placed by the dramatist that the speaker's meaning is overtaken, in the very utterance, by contextual meaning.

The word 'wounds' is used obsessively in *Coriolanus* (where, by a different paradox, it becomes part of the currency of political canvassing). Alcibiades refers at III. v. 67 to wounds 'plenteous' not sustained by his friend but inflicted by him (there is a fugitive cross-reference to the major theme of munificence in the adjective 'plenteous'). As the realisation grows in him that his plea has been refused – with, as Alcibiades sees it, an implication of personal insult, he begins to substitute his own desert for that of his friend. Afterwards, when the word 'wounds' occurs again, it means, as in *Coriolanus*, wounds sustained by the hero:

Alcib. I cannot think but your age has forgot me;

> It could not else be I should prove so base,
> To sue and be denied such common grace.
> My wounds ache at you.
>
> (III. v. 93–6)

By accident of time and usage it may be that the last phrase is more powerful today than it was in Shakespeare's time. As the New Arden editor notes, the same phrase occurs in Middleton's *A Chaste Maid in Cheapside* but this of itself scarcely constitutes strong evidence for Middleton's hand at this point, since the phrase may be proverbial. Certainly a version of it can be found in *Coriolanus* – the 'unaching scars' at II. ii. 148. Yet the poetry works here, perhaps, by reactivating trite language. 'Common grace' at line 95 has the low-key, secular meaning, 'ordinary decency', but 'grace' is, as we shall see, a term of power in *Timon*, in which the deeper religious signification is latent, waiting to be brought into play. Even here the language, even if unremarkable on the surface, is beginning to resonate with further significance. In much the same way the notion of redemption through blood is lurking behind lines 84–5.

In general, Alcibiades' presence in the play has the effect of matching the structures of economic discourse, not with those of the higher morality, but with physical blood and death. In I. ii, we saw Timon strangely fascinated by the man of blood, whose feasting is on enemies (75) and whose living is among the dead (222–3). Here Alcibiades offers to 'pawn' his own victories on his friend's behalf. E. R. Dodds in a lecture on Aeschylus' *Agamemnon* once observed that in primitive Greek society a killing must always be answered by another killing, until we come to the happy moment when money is invented, at which point a death-price, like the Saxon *wergeld*, can be exacted instead of another human life, and so at last the chain is broken. Alcibiades' language seems to move weirdly in a limbo between the two conceptions of justice, the pre-economic and the economic. The actual legal situation is, as it happens, primitive. His friend's life is forfeit and to offer money to buy it back would be bribery. Yet Alcibiades seems to scent the possibility of redeeming the art of bribery by substituting the blood of others for money. It is as if he thinks that war service is in general equivalent to money since it can serve as a substitute value or medium of exchange, but also more narrowly, that in this way the 'dark' primal requirement of blood for blood is satisfied by his suggestion:

> If by this crime he owes the law his life,
> Why, let the war receive't in valiant gore,
> For law is strict, and war is nothing more.
>
> (III. v. 84–6)

Again the plea fails and Alcibiades, like Coriolanus, is banished. After all our strictures of Alcibiades, we may well think the penalty extreme. He is banished perpetually because he is angry at the refusal of his suit on behalf of a friend. Left alone on the stage, he now separates his world of warlike prowess from the world of finance:

> I'm worse than mad: I have kept back their foes.
> While they have told their money, and let out
> Their coin upon large interest; I myself
> Rich only in large hurts.
>
> (III. v. 107–10)

He vows a revenge which is like the original drunken quarrel which brought down his friend, but now enlarged with the full grandeur of projected war.

> Soldiers should brook as little wrong as gods.
>
> (III. v. 118)

Men of war do not submit tamely to insults. The last word of all may remind us of Coriolanus. Cominius said of him:

> He leads them like a thing
> Made by some other deity than Nature.
>
> (IV. vi. 90–1)

In *Coriolanus* the hero-god was unpolitical, unassimilable by a civil society. We may remember Aristotle's observation at *Politics*, 1253a, that the unsocial man is either a god or a beast (in *Timon* the word substituted for 'beast' is 'dog'). Alcibiades in his own way, which is very different from that of the dog Apemantus, has declared himself opposite to humanity.

In Plutarch's *Life of Antony* the link between the philosophic and the martial misanthrope is completed. Plutarch's Alcibiades is of course the historical Alcibiades, the beautiful, brilliant aristocrat, thought by many to have been corrupted by the philosophical teaching of Socrates, the man who betrayed his city. At the same time, however, this figure seems in Plutarch to be progressively involved in a web of myth. Plutarch says that Timon hated everyone except Alcibiades, whom he made much of and 'kissed very gladly'.[61] When asked why, he said it was because he knew Alcibiades would be the ruin of Athens. This account of the Cynic philosopher, kissing and making much of Alcibiades, reads like a curious reversed echo of the passage in Plato's *Symposium* (219B) where Alcibiades recounts how he embraced the philosopher Socrates in an effort to seduce him – but Socrates was interested only in talking about philosophy. In the Plato story erotic love is frustrated by the higher philosophy. In Plutarch, the love and the misanthropic philosophy are paradoxically made one. Plutarch's Timon loves Alcibiades as the agent of his own velleities: Timon can hate the world but Alcibiades can go one better: he kills. Shakespeare (or Middleton), surprisingly, either avoids or misses this strong knitting of the two themes, giving us only the faint echo in I. ii. Timon, even before his misanthropy began (or was uncovered), was drawn to the destructive genius of Alcibiades. Later, at IV. iii. 110, Timon in the wilderness grimly approves Alcibiades' plan to sack Athens, but keeps up nevertheless his stream of abuse: 'Confounded be thyself! Speak not, be gone' (IV. iii. 130). It is not enough to view the Alcibiades motif, half-assimilated though it is, in the rosy light of Jacobean nostalgia for the good old ways. Rather we have in Timon's reaction in I. ii the groundwork of a brilliant dramatic counterpointing, an admirable psychological anticipation of the way Timon will go; but the sketch is never finished.

III. vi opens with the entry of various Senators and friends of Timon, variously bemused. There is a conscious blankness about the presentation which, even if it proceeds from a different pen, successfully recalls the manner of the opening scene. This also is drama of the profile rather than of the full face. The friends have received their invitations to dinner and are hastily revising their strategy: what if Timon's seeming ruin had all been an elaborate pretence designed to test their loyalty? There may be a faint smell of dramatic reflexiveness here. Sequences in which one person subjects another to intolerable psychological pressure and then suddenly smiles and says 'I did this but to try thee' recur in the drama of the period. Indeed one supposes – or hopes – that the pattern is more strongly established in drama than it can ever have been in life. The effect of this is to make the Senators sound in a way like seasoned play-goers, smelling out the likely course of the plot. But then they are *in* the plot and must take immediate measures.

The opening exchange is brief, but long enough to suggest a serious lack of practical ideas. The entry of Timon is – beautifully – an *interruption* not of their plans but of a manifest inability to plan. Timon greets them warmly and there is a general forcing of smiles. The Second Lord's image at III. vi. 28–9 is ill judged, almost, indeed, a 'Freudian slip'. He says that summer is not more welcome to the swallow than Timon is to his friends. The suggestion of 'fair weather friends' is inescapable (though the New English Dictionary does not trace the phrase earlier than the eighteenth century and neither M. P. Tilley nor R. W. Dent can find it in the Shakespearean period), and indeed Timon at once moralises it in exactly this way, but in an 'aside'. The Lords may freeze into immobility as Timon speaks and then resume their lives, having heard nothing. Incidentally the association of birds and summer is very characteristic of Shakespeare. Although Timon might have permitted it, the Lords dare not proceed as if nothing has happened. The First Lord can think of no posture but one of abject apology, but nevertheless essays a light tone:

> I hope it remains not unkindly with your lordship that I return'd you an empty messenger.
>
> (III. vi. 35–6)

Timon reassures him and there is a sudden general feeling of relief. In these circumstances the Second Lord feels that he can afford to be more effusive in his apology:

> My most honourable lord, I am e'en sick of shame, that when your lordship this other day sent to me I was so unfortunate a beggar.
>
> (III. vi. 40–3)

'Beggar' looks for a moment like a mistake for 'beggee' (had such a word existed) but the Lord presumably means by 'beggar' simply 'pauper' or 'wretched fellow'. Those with no fears about over-reading texts may find, nevertheless, an appropriate psychological confusion in the mild oddity of the word (appropriate, because the Lord is and knows himself to be a parasite on Timon). Freudian slips, as we have seen, *are* in the air.

The question may be raised whether Timon, in effect, lies at this point in the play. The creditors are obviously anxious that he may hold their behaviour against them. His answers are clear signals that he will not. It might be thought that a principled hero, intending revenge, would have avoided answering. Is this a sign that the change in Timon, from love to enmity, is accompanied by a more extensive moral inversion? The old Timon would have regarded such deception as beneath the proper magnanimity of a gentleman. Yet Timon's words *are* formally non-committal. He simply instructs both lords to stop thinking, which is, very exactly, what is required at this point by Timon, the impresario of surprise. The point is thus a fine one, but the element of deception is inescapable and indeed marks a fundamental shift of some kind – perhaps, though this may sound odd, in the direction of Timon, the humorist. Certainly, Timon is not generous in his hatred as he was generous in his love (I use the word 'generous' here with a sense of its etymological link with the notion of lineage and nobility). The larger figures of deceived generosity in Shakespeare – Othello, Lear, Coriolanus – would all strike back, but would not stoop to practical jokes. Even Antonio in *The Merchant of Venice*, for all that the play is a comedy, could not conceivably do such a thing, though Portia can, on his behalf.

The lords begin to talk excitedly about Alcibiades' banishment. It is noteworthy that Timon plays no part in this dialogue. It is almost an instance of a significant dramatic silence, though Timon is not directly addressed. The bland, blank smile must remain on the actor's face. The audience at the first performance did not know for sure at this point what Timon was up to. But then the sharper wits would not have believed the words of the Second Lord (who may indeed be cheering himself up): 'This is the old man still' (III. vi. 60). Certainly the Third Lord is less confident: 'Will't hold? Will't hold? (III. vi. 61).

They sit. Timon says Grace (of which more in another place). The dishes are uncovered, revealing lukewarm water. Timon throws the water over the guests and drives them from the table and the stage, cursing them. He then turns, like a figure in a Morality Play, to address the audience, but with the third-person, heroic, profile-grammar of the Roman plays:

> Burn, house! Sink, Athens! Henceforth hated be
> Of Timon, man and all humanity.
>
> (III. vi. 100–1)

Timon has turned the tables on the false friends. He has had his joke, perfected his revenge. But, we are told formally, this public reversal springs from a darker revolution within Timon himself. Here he proclaims himself a misanthrope.

The external action of the scene is more comedic than tragic. Until Timon's soliloquy it almost suggests sheer high spirits. The scene in Marlowe's *Doctor Faustus* in which the hero upsets the Papal banquet is in fact embedded comedy (and may well be by another hand than Marlowe's). There remains that intermediate ground, lying between life and art, the Elizabethan revel. The sudden, theatrical transformation of the dinner, a mixture of brilliant display with a kind of magnificent practical joke, figured in real feasts of the period. As there were anti-masques, so there were ante-suppers. The fashion was started apparently by a group including the handsome James Hay, who became as time went by first Viscount Doncaster, then Earl of Carlisle:

> . . . The Earl of Carlisle was one of the quorum that brought in the vanity of ante-suppers, not heard of in our forefather's time, and, for ought I have read, or at least remember, unpractised by the most luxurious tyrants. The manner of which was, to have the board covered, at the first entrance of the ghests, with dishes, as high as a tall man could well reach, filled with the choycest and dearest viands sea or land could afford: And all this once seen, and having feasted the eyes of the invited, was in a manner throwne away, and fresh set on to the same height, having only this advantage of the other, that it was hot.[62]

We do not know whether the food was really thrown away[63] or whether the phrase 'in a manner' implies some reservation (for example, there may have been a great show made of throwing the food away but it may afterwards have gone to the servants). We have not quite reached the point in competitive waste reached by the

American Indian potlatch, but it is not far off.

Hay's ante-supper, grotesquely whipped away from the expectant guests, was designedly followed by a feast which was better still. The intention is to be read as benign, though the element of showing off is hypertrophied to the point where the final effect is of enormous egoism rather than genuine benevolence. And perhaps this too, in an age in which the Sovereign, having neither a standing army nor a serious police force,[64] chose to exert power through display, was designed. Such behaviour must always have been more frightening than lovable. Moreover such occasions can easily go wrong; as we say of children's parties, 'It will all end in tears.' It is a mistake to assume that the practices of older, more hierarchical societies always worked harmoniously, through some mystical affinity with the organic. Proxy-wooings, masqued gate-crashing of parties and the like are customs fraught with psychological and social danger. In the latter case the danger was doubtless part of the fun, but the danger nevertheless was there. Even when masques were framed to celebrate order and religion, so that the modern reader is moved to exclaim at the exemplary piety of the text, these could in performance break down in squalid or uproarious confusion. The most notorious example is the *Masque of Solomon and the Queen of Sheba*, performed before King James and Christian of Denmark at Theobalds in 1606, of which we possess Sir John Harington's account. On this occasion the Queen of Sheba upset 'wine, cream, jelly, beverage, cakes, spices and other good matters' over the King, who rose at this and attempted to dance with her. This proved to be beyond James's powers; he fell and was carried to an inner chamber. Faith, Hope and Charity then appeared. Hope was too drunk to speak her lines, Faith was scarcely able to stand but Charity put up some sort of show before returning to rejoin Faith and Hope, 'who were both sick and spewing in the lower hall'.[65]

Festive rituals do not always enforce a stable hierarchy.

The energy of Elizabethan and Jacobean masquings and revels, like the energy of the contemporary drama, springs from a dangerous, unprecedented mingling of order with disorder. We may seek to impose a retrospective stability on the whole field by speaking of 'safety-valves', 'controlled pseudo-subversion' or, conversely, of radical movements, but in truth the mixture seems to have been highly unstable, with no clear evidence of cool management (except for certain Court masques) by any political constituency. What is clear is that Timon's anti-feast would not be for the Jacobean audience the profoundly eccentric thing it is for us. Joke-dinners were familiar, and the *thought* of such a thing turning nasty must have occurred to many people on many occasions, since this is an important source of the excitement.

But when Timon *soliloquises* we realise that, because he hates mankind, he is attacking not just these individual persons but festivity itself. It is as if Malvolio ('Ill Will') were to take over the management of one of Hay's ante-suppers. We move from the comedic-anarchic to the antisocial (a weak term for a profound condition) and as we do so the stage, appropriately enough, clears, leaving one alone who is, in Aristotle's words, both more and less than man. He rages against Athens, and then departs.

Timon's exit is followed, with great dramatic art, by a brief explosion of superb comedy. The Lords and Senators re-enter, scrambling and searching for their hats and coats. We are admitted for a moment to a backstairs view. The indeterminate localisation of the Jacobean stage is here well used, so that we are no longer in the state apartments but find ourselves in the cloakroom (always of keen interest to parties of tourists going round great houses today). It is indeed almost as if the stage figuratively set by Timon *within* the fiction for his grand gesture is now reversed, showing the subsequent backstage confusion, though the analogy is imperfect, since the Lords were rather victims than actors in the earlier episode. The First Lord is in deeper trouble than the rest because he has lost not just a cap but a jewel, beaten from his hat by Timon who had formerly bestowed it. It is a measure of the general panic that, though the Second Lord finds his missing cap, the First Lord does not find the (much more valuable) jewel, but determines to leave nevertheless.

IV. i is a scene with a single character and a single speech. The speech, however, is a big one. Timon, *furibundus* still, pronounces his curse. Because he speaks not simply from hatred but from a subverted moral basis, he wishes on his fellow creatures not simply suffering but a general inversion of natural relations. Plagues, sciatica, itches, blains and general leprosy are to be visited on Athens, but that is not all. The ancient trope known in Greek as the *adynata* and in Latin as the *impossibilia*, whereby fishes find themselves in tree-tops and birds under the sea, is invoked as a figure of malediction. In ancient literature the trope of the world turned upside down was variously used to describe the Golden Age, to express ultimate absurdity or indeed, as in one of the earliest versions we have,[66] to convey a condemnation. Timon would have sober nations turn to lust, children to disobedience, all customs of religion and society 'Decline to your confounding contraries!' (IV. i. 20). The general bias of the incongruities is indeed firmly from good to bad. It is perhaps Timon's most Lear-like speech. Compare Lear's

> Strike her young bones,
> You taking airs, with lameness . . .
> . . . Infect her beauty,
> You fen-sucked fogs, drawn by the pow'rful sun,
> To fall and blister
>
> (II. iv. 163–8)

Timon's words at IV. i. 11–12,

> Large-handed robbers your grave masters are,
> And pill by law

have a potential political subversiveness. Here fierce

contrariety of mind reaches out towards and almost touches the practical contrariety of social revolution. Timon anticipates the famous watchword of later radicalism, 'Property is theft.' In *King Lear* there is, once more, a parallel with a difference. Lear in his madness came to see the magistrate as guiltier than the criminal, to see authority as violence. The passage in which this conversion happens is instinct with moral regeneration; Lear even in the depth of his madness is learning charity. There is no such implication of moral renewal in Timon's lines. At the same time the economic aspect, unstressed in *King Lear*, is foregrounded in *Timon*. Wilson Knight's contention that Timon differs from Lear in that he changes absolutely from perfect love to perfect hate[67] is strongly corroborated by this discrepancy in an otherwise parallel passage.

An odd note is struck in Timon's curse by the words,

> Bankrupts, hold fast;
> Rather than render back, out with your knives,
> And cut your trusters' throats.
>
> (IV. i. 8–10)

The passage is odd, first, because a bankrupt, by definition, cannot render back and, secondly, because of the sympathy given to the creditors, here called 'trusters'. Timon had his own trusters and he gave their money away to undeserving persons. The norm implied by Timon's insistence on absurdity is one in which bankrupts, *per impossibile*, pay their debts and satisfy their creditors; that is the opposite of the 'noble' ethic offered by J. W. Draper as central to the play and especially inapposite on the lips of Timon. Timon in this part of the play must believe himself to have been deeply wronged, the injured rather than the injurer. Yet these words imply a very different view. Words like 'ambiguity' and 'dialectic' which so often come to the critic's aid on occasions like this will not serve here. I can make no sense of it.

In the following scene the Steward and the servants review their own fortunes and the fall of Timon. They might have been forgiven had they expressed some resentment, but there is no breath of this. Presumably the object is to show how Timon is loved by those who work for him, though not by the objects of his liberality. For all that, one's credulity is a little strained by these pathologically loyal persons. The house is ruined and the servants are departing, to an indeterminate future. It is almost as if they say their farewells and then dislimn in air.

The Steward says he is as poor as they but at line 27 he gives money to each and his last words in the scene are 'Whilst I have gold, I'll be his steward still' (IV. ii. 51). It would have been easy to maintain the sentimental shape of the scene by avoiding all reference to any money the servants might have left, but that is not what we are given. The whole episode is a lyrical meditation on the drama of schematically reduced humanity from which we began; paralogically the characters almost sense the pathos of their own half-existence. The Steward, even amid the ruin of the house, must go on dispensing money because his identity is invested in his office: his *esse* is to dispense. It is as if, were he to cease to have gold, he would not only be Timon's Steward no longer, he would cease to exist. Lines 33–6,

> Who would be so mock'd with glory, or to live
> But in a dream of friendship,
> To have his pomp and all what state compounds
> But only painted like his varnish'd friends?

refer us back to the opening discussion of the painter's art, conducted by the abstract figures of Poet and Painter, themselves like painted persons on a wall.

The Steward gives us a new formula for Timon. Where before we were told that his giving was never ignoble but only foolish (II. ii. 178) we are now told that his one vice is an excess of goodness, something close to a logical absurdity yet at the same time enough to ruin him:

> Poor honest lord brought low by his own heart,
> Undone by goodness; strange, unusual blood,
> When man's worst sin is he does too much good.
>
> (IV. ii. 37–9)

The new version maintains the posture of moral loyalty to Timon, yet it now implicitly allows that generosity such as we witnessed in the first part of the play is not merely foolish; it is also exaggerated and in this exaggeration lay the germ of destruction. The Steward may seem to moralise with the simplicity of an older drama, but, as he speaks, the thought grows surprisingly intricate. We seem at first to have a mode in which moral exemplars are paraded to instruct the onlookers: 'Flee vice, or end like me.' But then, with a flicker of reflexive awareness, the Steward seems to become momentarily critical of the drama in which he figures. If Timon's vice was only an excess of virtue might not the audience be misled by the pattern set before them? Might they not assume, following the normal rules of the game, that they should do the opposite of what Timon did and therefore give up even the moderate charity they practised before?

> Who then dares to be half so kind again?
>
> (IV. ii. 40)

Instead of avoiding excess, they might avoid benevolence itself. The tolling bell of the Morality rings out with a cracked sound.

The single departing figure of the Steward is replaced, as we move to IV. iii, by the solitary figure of Timon 'in the woods'. We seem to have travelled back to the earliest period of Greek drama, in which the 'second actor' has not yet been invented and where, instead of to-and-fro dialogue, the same speaker came forward to address the audience in a succession of different masks. But while the Steward's isolation was accidental, Timon's is, so to speak, professional. He has gone out into the woods, while Apemantus has never moved.

· 8 ·

Timon in the Wilderness

We who live after the Romantics may have some difficulty in registering the right degree of shock at Timon's translation. We must begin with the simplest instincts. No one in 1607 thought it bliss to go, say, on a solitary walking holiday. No one drove mile after mile looking for a beach that was completely deserted. No one had himself painted as a tiny figure standing alone in an overwhelming, desolate landscape. In general it was felt to be more oppressive to be alone than to be in a crowd. Holidays, for the upper classes as much as for the lower, were spent in great throngs of people.

If one looks up the word 'alone' in a Shakespeare concordance one becomes aware very quickly that it is far more intimately linked with fear and anxiety than is the case today. One catches it in the almost childlike cry of the dying king in the Second Part of *Henry IV*, IV. v. 50, 'Why did you leave me here alone?' Speed in *Two Gentlemen of Verona* is moved to strong language by the spectacle of a person who desired 'to walk alone, like one that hath the pestilence' (II. i. 21–2). But Speed's energy of language is prompted by the presence of a challenge: he is describing a case of love-melancholy, by this date (1594?) a recognised pathological condition having at the same time a certain murky glamour about it. Near the beginning of *Romeo and Juliet* Romeo is similarly in love or infatuated.

Benvolio. Madam, an hour before the worshipp'd sun
Peer'd forth the golden window of the east,
A troubled mind drave me to walk abroad.
Where, underneath the grove of sycamore
That westward rooteth from the city side,
So early walking did I see your son.
Towards him I made, but he was ware of me,
And stole into the covert of the wood.
I, measuring his affections by my own,
Which then more sought where most might not be found,
Being one too many by my weary self,
Pursued my humour not pursuing his,
And gladly shunn'd who gladly fled from me.
Montague. Many a morning hath he there been seen,
With tears augmenting the fresh morning's dew,
Adding to clouds more clouds with his deep sighs,
But all so soon as the all-cheering sun
Should in the farthest east begin to draw
The shady curtains from Aurora's bed,
Away from light steals home my heavy son,
And private in his chambers pens himself,
Shuts up his windows, locks fair daylight out
And makes himself an artificial night.

(I. i. 118–40)

It is an extraordinary, and perhaps a seminal, passage. I suggest that the lines may be seminal, not because of the picture they offer of amorous solitude (this, after all, is Petrarchan), but because of their complex, haunting structure. The usual Elizabethan hostility to unsocial behaviour is sustained but with it a special fascination is created. A complex system of pre-echoes is set up. Benvolio, even while he reports the aberrant behaviour of the truant from society, reflects that aberrancy in his own milder disposition. He too had gone walking alone, he too nurses a troubled mind. Romeo's love is itself a mild pre-echo, within the play, of the love for Juliet which will follow. There is a faint sense, as Romeo retreats into the wood, that Benvolio is eluded by his double, that the subjective solitary pursues and loses the objective, the figure in the landscape. It is the element of fascination which grows in later literature, in the nocturnal delicious melancholy of Milton's *Il Penseroso*, in the fugitive Other Poet in the darkened churchyard of Gray's *Elegy*, in the ghostly scholar gypsy, hunted by Matthew Arnold through the deep fields of Oxfordshire.

Romeo sought a lover's solitude, while Timon has no love. Lovers, like holy fools, are accorded a certain indulgence by society, an indulgence not unmixed with awe. No such indulgence is available for Timon, whose solitude is squarely based not on love but hate. It follows that in his case reasons of a wider nature must be alleged. Of course amorous unsociability can on occasion adduce philosophical reasons in its own support, as when Pyrocles debates with Musidorus in Sidney's *Arcadia*. Pyrocles is in love and, like Romeo after him, retreats into the woods: '. . . every morning early going abroad either to the garden or to some woods towards the desert, it seemed his only comfort was to be without a comforter'.[68] Musidorus upbraids him and suggests that unsociability is flat contrary to virtue: 'You subject yourself to solitariness, the sly enemy that doth most separate a man from well-doing.'[69] Pyrocles' answer is that in solitude the mind aspires to higher thought:

> . . . the workings of the mind I find much more infinite than can be led unto by the eye, or imagined by any that distract their thoughts without themselves. And in such contemplation or, as I think, more excellent, I enjoy my solitariness, and my solitariness perchance is the nurse of these contemplations. Eagles we see fly

> alone, and they are but sheep which always herd together.[70]

Musidorus urges the moral claims of the active life and Pyrocles the intellectual merits of the contemplative.

The word 'contemplative' is enough to remind us that all the while there has existed an older, religious tradition of withdrawal from the world. Christ himself went out into the wilderness to wrestle with the devil. The Desert Fathers and the Hermits all turned their backs on a corrupt society. But Sidney's words are virtually without religious import. The contemplation treasured by Pyrocles is linked by its imagery of aspiration and flight to those Hermetical dreams of godlike knowledge which in the imagination of the period warred endlessly with Calvin's subjection of human nature to total depravity. Janette Dillon in *Shakespeare and the Solitary Man* observes that in the Middle Ages Aristotle's description of the unsocial man as either a god or a beast was interpreted as meaning that all solitude other than that sought for prayer and contemplation was sinful, but as we reach the seventeenth century we find increasingly the notion that solitude is good, not because it enables man to approach God, but because it enables man to become godlike through intellectual power. Sometimes indeed the point is made more modestly. Thus, Wye Saltonstall in his Character of 'A Melancholy Man' is content to suggest that solitude is associated with intelligence and contempt for mass opinion.[71] Janette Dillon also cites Cowley's words: 'Cogitation is the thing which distinguishes the Solitude of God from a wild Beast.'[72] Thus the strands begin to multiply under our fingers. Religious retreat can, by the tropes of courtly love, still working in the sixteenth century, lie behind amorous solitude and can, at the same time, be transformed by the Renaissance cult of the intellectual hero. The Renaissance in its turn will draw on varied classical sources, including Stoicism which (especially in the writings of Seneca) offers a philosophy of austere withdrawal from the corrupt values of the world. Remember here that Timon is a Cynic, and Cynics and Stoics are near akin.

It is tempting to say that the one element of important innovation in all this is the emphasis placed by Musidorus on public action in the world as the proper province of virtue, though even this is anticipated in a manner by Pericles' funeral oration, as we read it in Thucydides (II, 40); there it is observed that the politically-minded Athenians have little time for the man who austerely keeps himself to himself.

Certainly it is significant that in Sidney's *Arcadia* the case made for retreat is not only secular but also amoral. All the morality has been appropriated by the other party. Morality itself is becoming *essentially* public, social, political. This feeling is powerfully present in Sir Thomas Elyot's *The Boke named the Governour* (1531). Elyot grounds his conception of public service in metaphysical theory. Individuality is not a principle opposed to relation; rather, individuality is a product of relation. Thinghood, identity itself, depends upon relation. Without relation we have not a series of individuals but mere, unmeaning chaos:

> . . . take away ordre from all thynges what shulde than remayne? Certes nothynge finally, except some man wolde imagine eftsones *Chaos*: whiche of some is expound a confuse mixture. Also where there is any lacke of ordre nedes must be perpetuall conflicte: and in thynges subjecte to Nature nothynge of hym selfe onely may be norished; but whan he hath destroyed that where with he dothe participate by the ordre of his creation, he hym selfe of necessite muste than perisshe, whereof ensue the universall dissolution.[73]

Elyot's second argument, for conflict rather than chaos as the opposite of ordered participation, may be incompatible with his first. But for all that the passage drives powerfully forward.

Janette Dillon suggests that the sixteenth century in England saw an abrupt rise in the ideal of state service and a correlative displacement of religious retreat (doubtless assisted by Protestant mistrust of monasticism). Bacon, expounding the myth of Narcissus who fell in love with his own reflection, says that the reference is to those who are afraid to engage in public business and in consequence lead a 'solitary, private and shadowed life'.[74] This assertion of public active morality is immediately succeeded by a new cult of solitude, now quite separate from the religious ideal. Petrarch's *De Vita Solitaria* which Dillon carefully distinguishes as being secular from the same author's *De Otio Religioso* is a crucial early document. After about 1570 the affectation of melancholic isolation crops up more and more frequently. There seems to be some evidence that it emerges first in Court circles and then spreads to the surrounding society. Literature, viewing this modish behaviour from outside, at first sees it as foolish or comic. We may think here of Armado in *Love's Labour's Lost* or of Macilente in Jonson's *Every Man Out of his Humour* (1599). Macilente begins the play by promising to outdo Stoic and Cynic alike in his contempt for the world. In *As You Like It* Orlando is set, as an index of health, beside the sick affectation of Jaques. 'I am glad of your departure', says Orlando, 'Adieu, good monsieur Melancholy' (III. ii. 293). The audience is expected to concur with Orlando's judgement, even though (and this is itself important) they might nevertheless wish to detain Jaques on the stage for his entertainment value. Lodovico in *The White Devil* (III. iii. 79) speaks contemptuously of 'gentle' (that is, 'upper-class') melancholy and of going unwashed and lousy but with underclothes of finest taffeta. Robert Greene says that he affected the melancholy in his youth.[75] Nashe, who, like Greene, established himself in London, suggests, with a hermetical emphasis on the exciting idea of a secret élite, that the cult of solitude, so far from being the opposite of the political, could itself be used to a political end, though he allows that the idea is in a manner absurd:

> Some think to be counted rare politicians and statesmen by being solitary; as who should say, 'I am a wise man, a brave man, *Secreta mea mihi; Frustra sapit, qui sibi non sapit* [My secrets are for me; his wisdom is vain, who is not wise to himself] and there is no man worthy of my company or friendship.'[76]

Janette Dillon further notes that Sir Thomas Overbury's Character of 'A Melancholy Man' is still traditionalist, condemning the solitary as a deviant from social order, but that John Earl's 'Contemplative Man' (1628) commends withdrawal for intellectual reasons; meanwhile sermons, as one might have expected, repeatedly condemn the cult of solitude.[77]

Dillon's study is both richly informed and immensely perceptive. Very occasionally one wonders whether the very writing of such a book predisposes the author to enlist passages too readily on one side or the other, *pro* or *contra*. Jaques is indeed hated in *As You Like It* but it is equally clear that Shakespeare respects him. Dillon says of Timon:

> Like Coriolanus and Macbeth, Timon cuts himself off from society, and the perspective of collective absolutes reasserts itself beyond the life of the individual. The solitary, in reflecting the framework of natural absolutes which binds him, destroys not the framework but himself.[78]

This is just but it is not the whole story. That Timon must become a moral outcast, must secede from the society of human beings, must be destroyed, is all undisputed, common ground. But we are never allowed to be certain that he was wrong.

Julius Caesar explores a paradox of democracy; what happens if the people choose to live under tyrant, to resign their powers to him? What happens if the *dēmos*, by due democratic process, renders itself undemocratic?

Timon of Athens explores a similarly structured paradox of humane ethics: what happens if the human race, collectively, is inhumane? If ethical rules are derived from, and operate within, the interest of the species, the elimination of that species is not just wicked; it is also ethical nonsense. If on the other hand ethical judgements are absolute in the sense of being extra-social, it is not necessarily nonsensical to find a society, or even all societies, ethically wanting. Even the elimination of the human race becomes conceivable *as an ethical duty*. When D. H. Lawrence's Birkin thought the world would be a better place with the human beings gone and in their place just grass – with, somewhere, a hare sitting up – his motive, bizarre though this may seem, was ethical (*Women in Love*, ch. XI). Birkin is a sincere misanthrope. He is moved not by a wish to inflict pain but by a desire that horrible wickedness be removed from the face of the earth. By the former ethic misanthropy is the Primal Error; but, if we allow the proposition 'Mankind is disgusting', by the second ethic misanthropy is merely just. There is no doubt that in *Timon* the former ethic in general prevails, but the other is never quite allowed to die. Indeed, if it did, the drama would at once become much less interesting.

The speech of Ulysses on 'degree' in *Troilus and Cressida* (I. iii. 83–134) is very close in its phrasing to Sir Thomas Elyot's words in the passage I quoted from *The Governour* – so close that Elyot has been claimed as a specific source. Later in *Troilus and Cressida* Ulysses is given a speech of astonishing philosophical acuteness in which he suggests not only that moral action entails participation in society but that whenever we describe a person *in any way at all* we are forced to presuppose a relation to others; even introspection is a matter of public relationships. The atmosphere surrounding the speech is intellectual, sophisticated. To begin with, Ulysses is doing something his Homeric antecedent would never have done: he is *reading*. When Achilles enquires, for all the world like one don of another, what he is reading (afterwards he 'places' the answer he receives) Ulysses uses a phrase which catches exactly the tone of conversation among informed, highly literate people: 'I do not strain at the position – / It is familiar' (III. iii. 112–13). But then he presses on:

> . . . no man is the Lord of anything,
> Though in and of him there be much consisting,
> Till he communicate his parts to others;
> Nor doth he of himself know them for aught,
> Till he behold them formed in th' applause
> Where th'are extended: who, like an arch reverb'rate
> The voice again, or like a gate of steel,
> Fronting the sun, receives and renders back
> His figure and his heat.
>
> (III. iii. 115–23)

Ulysses proposes at once the most rhetorically majestic and the most metaphysically acute rationale for public action in a hierarchical society. Yet the context of the play infects everything he says with moral dubiety. His emphasis on relations can, by a mere change in the shading, be transformed into the merest Pyrrhonism (that is, radical scepticism). Indeed, Pyrrho himself put an argument very like that offered by Ulysses when he said that 'No single thing is in itself any more this than that'. Thus far Shakespeare's Ulysses would agree and so perhaps would Sir Thomas Elyot; but Elyot would never have accepted Pyrrho's sceptical conclusion: 'And so there is nothing really existent, but custom and convention govern human action.'[79] This, it will be said, is not made explicit in *Troilus and Cressida*. But the play does contain the celebrated dispute between Troilus and Hector in which Troilus asks the Pyrrhonian question, 'What's aught but as 'tis valued?' (II. ii. 52) while Hector – until his notorious *volte-face* – maintains the notion of intrinsic value. The position taken by Troilus is presented as a very doubtful mixture of chivalric enthusiasm and radical scepticism.

Thus Ulysses is subtly undermined first by the obvious moral hollowness of the society he serves and secondly by the sense in the play of a dangerous implicit connection between relationalism (respectable) and relativism (the reverse).

Thus even those notions which look like 'bedrock' ideas, underpinning the fabric of society, can, in the hands of a dramatist like Shakespeare, prove fluid, live, shifting things. Ulysses in his speech on 'degree' found a hierarchical benevolence in the Sun:

> . . . therefore is the glorious planet Sol
> In noble eminence enthron'd and spher'd
> Amidst the other; whose med'cinable eye
> Corrects the [ill aspects] of [planets evil] . . .
>
> (I. iii. 89–92)

Timon, with a converse intention, also calls upon the sun:

> O blessed breeding sun draw from the earth
> Rotten humidity; below thy sister's orb
> Infect the air!
>
> (IV. iii. 1–3)

He does not, as one might expect, invite the sun to run headlong from the sky, inverting cosmic hierarchy. In a curious way his language is more modest, more realistic than that. Rather he exploits a perfectly ordinary, empirical sense that the sun can be as easily an agent of disease as of health, that it is as congenial to his office to rot things as to ripen them. In *Antony and Cleopatra* it is the sun that fertilises the slime and ooze of the Nile, engendering serpents and crocodiles (II. vii. 22–7), as in Spenser's *Faerie Queene*, where we read that men find infinite shapes of creatures in the Egyptian sand 'on which the Sunne hath shynd' (III. vi. 8). Even in a northern country the sun is not automatically seen as benevolent. London must have smelled worse in summer than in winter.

Timon wishes at once to cling to and to invert the idea of Nature. Nature, he says, can bear great fortune only by contempt of nature; that is, humanity is such that only inhumanity will protect the outstanding man, the person especially exposed. He then moves, however, to a more conventional invocation of the World Turned Upside Down. Again the words are like and unlike what we find in *King Lear*. When the old, mad King wants to change round the beadle and the whore he whips (IV. vi. 160–2), neither love nor justice is utterly despaired of. So to invert is really to restore a more fundamental propriety. Behind all stands the scriptural text, 'He hath put down the mighty from their seats, and exalted them of low degree' (*Luke* 1: 52). Timon's words follow this pattern:

> The senators shall bear contempt hereditary,
> The beggar native honour.
> It is the pasture lards the brother's sides,
> The want that makes him lean.
>
> (IV. iii. 10–13)

The last two lines quoted probably mean, 'One brother grows fat on inherited land, the other wastes away in penury.' This is a reference to a feature of the existing social order which is treated with real moral indignation at the beginning of *As You Like It* (I. i. 1–25). Yet here the appetite for comprehensive chaos blots out everything else. Even the brilliant satirical touch of 'the learned pate / Ducks to the golden fool' (IV. iii. 17–18) somehow loses its edge as it is uttered. Where misanthropy is as universal as Timon's there can be no indignation at *specific* evils, no thought of corrective reform, but only of destruction.

Timon, more beast than god, turns from humanity to dig like Caliban for roots in the earth. One almost wishes that Shakespeare had caused Timon to dig with his bare hands rather than with a spade (IV. iii. 207). In any case we can require, in production, a hunched, bent figure, itself presenting a marked contrast with the erect posture of the gentleman. What we are given is almost the image of Nebuchadnezzar in the Bible, who 'did eat grass as oxen'. The picture in *Daniel* 4: 33 is a strong one; the

King of Babylon crawls in the fields, wet with dew, his hair like feathers, his nails like claws.

Timon in digging for roots finds gold. Suddenly he is rich again in the thing that ruined him. This time he resolves that he will not be a victim but will rather ally himself with the destroyer, gold, will co-operate in the ruining of others:

> I will make thee
> Do thy right nature –
>
> (IV. iii. 44–5)

If money is to destroy and corrupt as Timon wishes, it must circulate. But as he hears the drum of the approaching Alcibiades his first instinct is the low, commonplace impulse to hide what he has found. The bestial Timon, after all, must have wished to live, because he wished to eat; otherwise he would not have dug for roots; in like manner this half-infantile, Caliban-like second self will hug its property to itself to conceal it from prying eyes.

When Alcibiades enters Timon either pretends not to recognise him or really does not. Again, the universality of his misanthropy obliterates distinctions. But he confesses their acquaintance as he recognises the Blood-letter; this man can be employed to kill all the others.

The encounter between the two men is watched by two women: rouged, corrupt figures. One can imagine the scene as painted by Cranach. The diseases they carry on their lips, Timon observes, have greater destructive power than Alcibiades bears in his sword (IV. iii. 63–5). If Timon remains on the ground the presence of these will accentuate the bizarre humiliation of his posture. It is a picture of deliberately unpleasing decorative ingenuity, in which an ill light is shed on everyone present. Those who wish to maintain that Alcibiades in the central part of the play is the noble soldier may here claim that his character is now simply reversed, from good to evil, like Timon's, and that we are now presented with the other side. But the continuities in Alcibiades are too strong: he was always bent on death, while now, flanked by his whores, he is still capable of magnanimity towards Timon. When Alcibiades asks what act of friendship he can offer Timon, he receives the inwardly weak answer, 'None, but to maintain my opinion' (IV. iii. 72). It is as if Timon, Iago-like, were momentarily conscious of the thinness of his new belief and is openly asking that his prejudice be corroborated. The corroboration he seeks is, to be sure, almost certainly of a practical kind; 'maintain' is a stronger word than is obvious to us in the twentieth century; Timon is expecting Alcibiades to maintain it by the sword.

Alcibiades offers Timon gold. We in the audience know that he has gold of his own, but Timon does not at once disclose the fact, parrying, as he parried over the recognition of Alcibiades earlier in the scene. Timon counters the economy of symbolised (monetary) wealth with prior economy of biological exchange: 'Keep it, I cannot eat it' (IV. iii. 102). The drama has by now accustomed us to this play of food against money. Yet it is difficult to assess the force of Timon's reply here. He switches to a more fundamental level but we cannot say, for example, that in doing so he embraces common sense or asserts basic realism. In a way his reply is almost idiotic. Money could buy him better food than roots. Timon's aggressive materialism is both infantile and, one senses, absurdly theatrical, wildly unrealistic. All the while we know of course that he really has gold and that he hopes to make use of it. Yet he seems oddly hesitant, to have lost direction and impetus. Alcibiades then explains that he is at war with Athens. If we remember our Plutarch,[80] we expect Timon to express joyous approval, but as it turns out there is no big reaction: Timon can almost be said to have muffed it:

Alcib. When I have laid proud Athens on a heap –
Tim. Warr'st thou 'gainst Athens?

So far so good. Timon's sudden, alert question causes the audience to sit up. But the dialogue continues:

Alcib. Ay, Timon, and have cause.
Tim. The gods confound them all in thy conquest,
And thee after, when thou hast conquer'd!
Alcib. [As surprised as if *he* had read Plutarch] Why me, Timon?
Tim. That by killing of villains
Thou wast born to conquer my country.
(IV. iii. 103–8)

It might be argued that Timon's immediate reinclusion of Alcibiades in his hatred is a powerful reminder of the comprehensiveness of his misanthropy, but, as worded, it seems hardly to produce that effect, followed as it is by the lame, childishly conventional 'because you'd be conquering *my* country'. Timon answers in this way partly because his mind is distracted; he is thinking of his own gold. A possible moment of high rhetoric is here sacrificed to an extreme naturalism. Timon freezes, and then convulsively produces the treasure. The *action* is of course amazing – and excellent theatre – but the *language* is at first numb and then broken, mirroring the sub-rational, half-inadvertent character of the action:

Put up thy gold. Go on. Here's gold. Go on.
(IV. iii. 109)

The repeated 'Go on' marks the overriding of a strong but unspoken reaction from Alcibiades. Then, as Timon produces the gold, the flood of rhetoric is released with it and the joy in Athens's destruction which we looked for earlier now finds copious expression.

There is a touch of Lear's madness in:

Pity not honour'd age for his white beard:
He is an usurer. Strike me the counterfeit matron:
It is her habit only that is honest,
Herself's a bawd. Let not the virgin's cheek
Make soft thy trenchant sword: for those milk paps,
That through the window-bars bore at men's eyes,
Are not within the leaf of pity writ . . .
(IV. iii. 113–19)

Lear says:

> The usurer hangs the cozener.
> Through tatter'd clothes small vices do appear;
> Robes and furr'd gowns hide all.
>
> (IV. vi. 163–5)

Yet again we must register both likeness and unlikeness. The idea of vice peeping through seemingly virtuous barriers or of clothes hiding a vicious reality is present in both. The same imagery in some sort is working in the poet's mind. Indeed a little earlier in this scene from *King Lear* we also have 'white beard', in the shattering, surrealist line, 'Goneril with a white beard?' (IV. vi. 96). In *Timon* a stronger sexuality is permitted in the strange line about breasts seen through bars and the transition from usury to sexuality is more deeply embedded in the thematic structure of the play. In *King Lear* the usurer comes in almost incidentally; the analogous transition there is from familial ingratitude to an intuition of sexual corruption (IV. vi. 111–28). Yet even so the structure of that analogy is less evident. Perhaps we should say that in both plays there is a counterpointing of moral ingratitude with sexual vice, but in *Timon* the two are linked by usury, that third medium of corrupt exchange. I am arguing for a greater conceptual tightness in *Timon*. I concede, of course, the greater human, poetic and dramatic power of *Lear*.

Alcibiades coolly accepts the gold but not all the advice (IV. iii. 131). Again the effect is to make Timon's ravings seem unreal. Lear is never upstaged in this way. Alcibiades accepts the money with what we may call an inverse high-mindedness. His commitment to destruction is principled. Phrynia and Timandra take theirs from simple greed. This allows Shakespeare to produce a further, minor variation on the theme of equivalence: brute, biological facts underlying the symbolic patterns of civilised society. It is as if Alcibiades were a force of art, they a force of nature.

Timon catches this when he says:

> You are not oathable,
> Although I know you'll swear, terribly swear
> Into strong shudders and to heavenly agues
> Th'immortal gods that hear you. Spare your oaths:
> I'll trust to your conditions. Be whores still.
> (IV. iii. 137–41)

To say that someone is not 'oathable' is to say that the machinery of oath-swearing and undertaking is simply inoperable in such a case. Phrynia and Timandra, Timon is saying, exist below the network of civilised obligations and, although they may parrot oaths, their promises have no more significance than if they had indeed been uttered by irrational birds. What *can* be relied on is their physical function, the spreading of sickness and death. This Timon is happy to fund. There is indeed a more perfect 'fit' with his own views than he could ever hope to arrive at with Alcibiades. They have no pretensions to high principle and Timon can therefore do business, so to speak, with their *natures*, without impediments of art. As the transaction is completed, they, like Alcibiades, refer to the mixture of gold and advice, but, unlike him, express no intellectual reservation:

> More counsel with more money, bounteous Timon.
> (IV. iii. 169)

Alcibiades and his companions leave. Timon, once more alone, falls to his digging again. He calls upon the earth as the womb of all life to wither away and bring forth no more human progeny. The sense of death-wish grows strong again – death wished not only upon the rest of mankind but upon Timon himself. The notion once more is partly carried by the physical posture. Timon hacks at the ground as if struggling to re-enter what he himself calls a womb. The Old Man in Chaucer's *Pardoner's Tale*, desiring to end *his* life, beat upon the earth crying

Leeve Mooder, leet me in!

(731)

But Timon is still looking for food. The lines seem crossed: on the one hand the primal, almost healthily appetitive beast with the sick misanthrope. For half a line, in the heart of a play which turns, as we shall see, on the notion of perverted Grace-before-meat, Timon gives sincere thanks for ordinary bodily sustenance.

O, a root; dear thanks!

(IV. iii. 194)

The words are no sooner uttered than the gratitude is perverted by the misanthropy. In effect, Timon switches to gratitude for the fact that the root is *not* nourishing, for the next line calls for the obliteration of all juicy, rich foods, 'marrows, vines . . . / Whereof ingrateful man, with liquorish drafts / And morsels unctuous, greases his pure mind . . .' (IV. iii. 195–7).

Timon is not alone for long (though the lyric force of his soliloquy at IV. iii. 178–98 can if carefully managed create an effect of time suspended). Apemantus enters, exchanges curses and is driven off with stones, to be followed by the Banditti, then the Steward, then the Poet and Painter and then, in culmination, the Senators, who plead with Timon, urging him to return to Athens, that Alcibiades may be driven off and the city saved. All this may strike the reader as dangerously close to unintended comedy; the entrance to Timon's cave seems more like Paddington Station in the rush hour than a waste and desert place, far from all human taint. But to read so is to read in too naturalistic a way. A good production can bring out the proper effect, which is what we noted at the beginning, a mannered alienation. I emphasised there the resemblance to figures in profile, in an ancient frieze. Here, still more, the structure and character of the scene is astonishingly Greek.

It must be understood that I here press an analogy and

make no claims for direct influence. We have the pattern of the humiliated hero, apart from society, in a wild place. To him come, in succession, various figures to upbraid him or (more importantly) to solicit his aid. It is a pattern of great power in Sophocles, strong in Aeschylus, less strong in Euripides. In *Oedipus at Colonus* the protagonist, blind, filthy and ragged (1258–9), is visited in turn by Theseus, Creon and by Polynices, who wishes to raze Thebes to the earth in vengeance for the wrong he has suffered. Oedipus, for all his strange aura of sanctity, is more like Timon than one expects. He embraces his own wretchedness and curses those who have wronged him (91–3). We may think also of Aeschylus' *Prometheus Bound* (if the play is indeed his) in which the shackled hero is visited by Oceanus and Io, or of Sophocles' *Philoctetes*, in which the main character, *physically* offensive to society because of the smell from his wounded foot, is courted on his desolate island, in turn, by the reluctant Neoptolemus and the coldly realistic Odysseus, because without his bow Troy can never be taken. This mode of dramatic writing is heavily reproduced in Milton's *Samson Agonistes*. There the scheme is as follows: (1) Samson, humiliated; (2) To him, in turn, Manoa, Dalila, Harapha. Shakespeare's emphasis is, however, much less obtrusive than Milton's. Moreover we miss entirely in *Timon* the final, unearthly movement upward again, which informs the Sophoclean and Miltonic examples. Timon goes out, not into glory, but into air, water, nothingness.

The succession of exchanges, though harshly episodic in character, is artfully varied. Apemantus' manner is kindly, almost patronising (though there is some hostility in it). He, the veteran in misanthropy, chooses to see Timon's condition as an accidental malaise:

> This is in thee a nature but infected,
> A poor unmanly melancholy sprung
> From change of future.
>
> (IV. iii. 204–6)

Rowe in 1709 emended the Folio reading 'change of future' to 'change of fortune', a phrase which must have struck him as satisfyingly Aristotelian in tone. But it is seldom wise to substitute a commonplace for an unusual expression. A copyist would be most unlikely to transcribe the entirely predictable 'fortune' as 'future', but 'future' meaning 'prospect' and perhaps carrying at the same time a reflexive reference to the impending resolution of the drama is highly effective.

One senses that Apemantus is partly moved by territorial instincts: Timon in adopting his manners has usurped his ground. He proffers himself as a sort of Tempter in the Wilderness: why doesn't Timon live in corrupt ease like everyone else? Surely a real Cynic would simply join the system; to dissociate oneself is in a way to cling to idealism. Then, switching his tack, Apemantus discovers a Lear-like vein of sensitivity to ultimate physical distress:

> Call the creatures
> Whose naked natures live in all the spite
> Of wreakful heaven, whose bare unhoused trunks,
> To the conflicting elements expos'd,
> Answer mere nature . . .
>
> (IV. iii. 229–33)

The word 'unhoused' occurs in *Othello* (I. ii. 26) and not in *King Lear*. But in *King Lear* we have 'houseless' at III. iv. 26 and 30, and it is the *Lear* passage, not the *Othello*, which is relevant here. Once more we see the strange, deliberate impoverishment of an originally moral poetry. Lear's pity for the poor, naked wretches becomes, on the lips of Apemantus, a needling taunt, one philosopher baiting another for his want of realism. Timon at first hardly bothers to answer. Apemantus, that most sociable of misanthropes, refuses to be put off and warms to his theme: Timon, unlike Apemantus, is a creature of time, subject to changing fortune and mood; anyone who swings so violently from extreme to extreme could easily swing back.

The tempter has moved close to the ear of the desolate man. In *King Lear* Edgar, in the strangest of all dramatic sequences, seems to urge the blinded Gloster to hurl himself from Dover Cliff, as the devil urged Christ to throw himself down from the high place (*Luke* 4: 9; *Matthew* 4: 5–6) and afterwards, in another assumed character, cries that he has just seen the devil himself standing where he (Edgar) stood – at Gloster's elbow (IV. vi. 11–72). Note that in both the Gospel accounts we have, as a temptation, the idea of turning bread into stones; Timon at his mock banquet served stones instead of bread, reversing the scriptural story. Apemantus (less than diabolical) at the ear of Timon (less than Christ-like) begins to speak of death as the one sure escape from the giddy motion of life.

> Thou shouldst desire to die, being miserable.
> (IV. iii. 250)

Most of Timon's replies in this scene are brutish or infantile, but here he is strong in answer. It is precisely because he has known *difference*, variation in fortune, that his sufferings are palpable, his hate grounded. Duke Senior in *As You Like It*, a good structuralist before his time, finds reality in 'the season's difference'; harsh winters and cold winds are 'counsellors / That feelingly persuade me what I am' (II. i. 6–11). That there should be a kinship in Shakespeare's imagination between Duke Senior and Timon is not obvious, and yet it seems to be so. Both have been soft-living men, both find themselves suddenly translated to the wilderness, though in the comedy the wilderness is instantly recuperated for festive, courtly pastoral. Both are visited by an imperfectly explained hostility directed at a figure of melancholy, Jaques in *As You Like It*, Apemantus in *Timon*. In either play the stock melancholic figure is, against the natural expectation of the audience, accused of lust. I have already noted a shadowy connection between Jaques and Apemantus, hinted in the manner of Apemantus' entry in I. i. Now that connection grows stronger. Duke Senior says,

> . . . thou thyself hast been a libertine,
> As sensual as the brutish sting itself.
>
> (III. vii. 65–6)

Timon says to Apemantus,

> . . . thou wouldst have plung'd thyself
> In general riot, melted down thy youth
> In different beds of lust . . .
>
> (IV. iii. 257–9)

The accusation carries no objective force. The audience looking at the Cynic Apemantus will have little reason to believe him a frustrated rake. Yet Timon's and Duke Senior's words are full of power; they may fail to *describe* the object convincingly, but they *express* much that is vividly present in the speaking subject. Indeed there is one point in *As You Like It* where Shakespeare seems very strangely to have his lines crossed with various dramas as yet unwritten. Duke Senior says of Jaques,

> I think he be transform'd into a beast,
> For I can no where find him like a man.
>
> (II. vii. 1–2)

This, of the mannered, over-articulate Jaques! The line seems to have strayed into the play from *Timon* or from the Caliban scenes in *The Tempest*, in both of which the beast imagery is thoroughly integrated thematically. The Aristotelian equation of the unsocial man with the beast, germinally present in *As You Like It*, is developed in the later works.

Meanwhile the pastoral paradox of *As You Like It* whereby the rusticated court is momentarily seen as itself usurping the commonwealth of beasts reappears in *Timon* in an altered form. Duke Senior, about to hunt the deer, is whimsically irked by the thought that

the poor dappl'd fools,
Being native burghers of this desert city,
Should in their own confines with forked heads
Have their round haunches gor'd.

(II. i. 22–5)

Even as he envisages a pastoral radicalism more fundamental than any normally offered (upholding, against civilisation, not just the rights of shepherds but also even the rights of animals) the thought is silently transposed as in a mirror image: the ultra-pastoral beasts become civil ('burghers') while the human hunters become, by implication, wild, barbaric intruders; the oxymoron, 'desert city' is brilliantly pivotal. It is the regular fate of Duke Senior to express radical sentiments in terms which ironically reassert the claims of civility. In *Timon* Apemantus says, 'The commonwealth of Athens is become a forest of beasts' (IV. iii. 349–50). Duke Senior's observation is now reversed once more. The city of Athens is bestial, therefore the desert is civil. For a similarly vertiginous play with paradigmatic criteria, compare Marvell's lines in *The Garden*:

Society is all but rude
To this delicious solitude.

The writing in this scene is everywhere laced with a special vitality of intellect. Take the tiny exchange between Apemantus and Timon over the key word 'use':

Apem. Here is no use for gold.
Tim. The best and truest;
For here it sleeps and does no hired harm.

(IV. iii. 292–3)

Apemantus intends the word in its basic sense: Timon cannot use his money where there are no shops, where there is nothing to buy. But Timon hears an extended meaning in the word, the usury beyond the use, and counters that meaning with the idea of unused, sleeping gold. As he does so he reifies a negation and this too in its own way looks forward to the imminent end. There the thought is implicit, as is usually the way with Shakespeare's intelligence. Here the meaning is given explicitly. In this half human, Hellenic scene of encounters and withdrawals, there is the one majestic formula, to which we continually recur, *telling* us, not *showing* us, what we are to think. Apemantus says, 'The middle of humanity thou never knowest, but only the extremity of both ends' (IV. iii. 301–2). The whole history of modern literary criticism predisposes us to resist such overt imperatives; the critic must always, in a certain sense, 'know better' than the dramatist. But to this one we must submit.

A procession of sculptured figures must be treated serially and, so far, I have stuck closely to the temporal succession of dramatic tableaux in *Timon of Athens*. But although the play is in some ways archaistic in its technique, it is not in fact archaic. The whole is informed by a synchronic consciousness of its own strangeness and is energised from within by a kind of dark, punning philosophy. The implied terms of this are: *gratitude*, *gratuitous*, *gratis*, *gratuity*, *gratiae*, *grace*, *charis*, *Eucharist*. This central conception requires analysis of another kind.

Part 2

Timon Says Grace
The Parodic Eucharist

Timon. You great benefactors, sprinkle our society with thankfulness. For your own gifts, make yourselves prais'd; but reserve still to give, lest your dieties be despis'd. Lend to each man enough, that one need not lend to another; for were your godheads to borrow of men, men would forsake the gods. Make the meat be belov'd, more than the man that gives it. Let no assembly of twenty be without a score of villains. If there sit twelve women at the table, let a dozen of them be as they are. The rest of your fees, O gods, the Senators of Athens, together with the common [lag] of people – what is amiss in them, you gods, make suitable for destruction. For these my present friends, as they are to me nothing, so in nothing bless them, and to nothing are they welcome.

(III. vi. 69–81)

This is the second time in this play that grace is said. In Act 1, Scene 2, Apemantus the Cynic says,

Immortal gods, I crave no pelf;
I pray for no man but myself.

Grant I may never prove so fond,
To trust man on his oath or bond;
Or a harlot for her weeping,
Or a dog that seems a-sleeping,
Or a keeper with my freedom,
Or my friends, if I should need 'em.
Amen. So fall to't:
Rich men sin, and I eat root.

(62–71)

The speech of Apemantus is marked by a certain sprightliness of style and metre; we are aware of it as a separate, formal performance. In the Folio it is even given a title, 'Apemantus Grace'. It is, of course, an anti-grace in so far as it is antisocial but there is, for all that, a certain gaiety in the execution. Like the Pharisee (*Luke* 18: 11) Apemantus thanks God that he is not as other men, but unlike the Pharisee he is caustically and ironically conscious of the oddity of his prayer. The stark clarity of the language is played off against an enjoyable unclarity of tone (irony/'kidding on the level', prayer/mock-prayer, self-dissociation/collusion). It is also pleasurably dangerous, one supposes. Even Socrates (the progenitor of this mode) may have functioned on occasion as a licensed fool before the citizens decided that he had better die. The speech has immediate and vivid force, both in the feigned society of the play and the real society of the theatre. But Timon's grace is not like this. It is uneasy on the ear and mind, a series of awkward and apparently unexciting manoeuvres. We may, if we wish, say that *Timon of Athens* is an unfinished play and that Shakespeare would have improved this speech; or we may simply blame Middleton, the weaker member of the hypothetical collaborative team (though Middleton could in fact write prose of the sprightliest sort). But first we should notice two things about the text as we have it. First, the dramatist needs – at least until the last sentence – a numbing effect of pseudo-discourse, a sort of 'blah-blah' before falling upon the food. This is necessary because, although we are at the pivotal point in the play, the participants must not tumble to the truth at once. Timon has invited his faithless friends to another banquet and is on the point of giving them stones instead of food ('if a son shall ask bread . . . will he give him a stone?' *Luke* 11: 11) but the surprise must be held back. Shakespeare sometimes has his characters act as surrogate artificers of the action. Rosalind stage-manages the conclusion of *As You Like It* and Prospero (with some difficulty) coaxes the events of *The Tempest* to their resolution, to meet a neo-classical deadline. So here, Timon, magician, priest, host, joker, contrives that the pivotal transition of the play, from philanthropy to misanthropy, should be diversified by a technique of overlapping: the behaviour of hospitality must be made to run on, just for a moment, after hospitality itself has died. The structure is that of a joke (practical jokes often hurt). Timon's grace is therefore uttered in a non-time, a space of pure suspense. All the interest has suddenly fled to the practical context, the *before* and *after* of Timon's words and therefore what is required is, so to speak, a temporary hypnosis. The speech *needs* to be uninteresting, or at least to seem so. But at the same time it is a formal prayer offered by the protagonist at the crossroads, all of which cries out for richness of content. By a remarkable technical feat the dramatist supplies both the required nullity and the richness. If the dramatist is Shakespeare, we may say that for once he is obliged to dissemble his genius, to disguise his wealth as rhetorical poverty, but the wealth is there.

The prayer known as 'grace before or after meat' seems to be naturally liable to various forms of sophistication. The radical giving of thanks (*gratias*) for food turns into the more theologically complex request for a blessing on the meal, as if some anxiety about the brutalism of mere eating has entered and, with it, a consequent impulse to make the whole business more high-minded. Finally the grace ceases to express thanks and instead contorts itself into a pious request for thankful feelings ('For what we are about to receive may the Lord make us truly thankful').

Of course grace before meat is more naturally liable to this transformation than grace after meat. While anticipatory thanks are in principle possible ('For what we are about to receive, we thank thee, O Lord') it is easy to see how, before the meal, the expression of thanks can turn into petitionary prayer. The *Apostolical Constitutions*, a collection of ecclesiastical law dating from the latter half of the fourth century AD, provide a form of grace which seems grossly physical in comparison with later versions – 'Lord . . . who givest food to all flesh, fill our hearts with joy and merriment'[1] – yet even here the object of this petition is not mere food (which is, however, kept firmly in view in the subordinate clause) but a state of convivial feeling. But such merriment itself is dangerously carnal and this too can prove a source of disquiet. In Shakespeare's own century we can watch such anxieties working themselves out. *The Primer set furth by the Kinges Majestie & his Clergie*, 1545, gives various graces, one of which reads as follows:

> O Lord Jesus Christ, without whom nothyng is swete nor savery, we beseche the to blesse us and our supper, and wyth thy blessed presence to chere our hertes, that in al our meates and drynkes, we may tast and savoure of the to thy honor and glorye.[2]

The note of conviviality is still there in 'chere our hertes' (though how much weaker than, say, the 'ut corda nostra exhilares' of the Brasenose College grace[3]) but 'tast and savoure' are so to speak, defused, by being turned into a metaphor for an essentially spiritual petition, interpenetrating the physical. What is tasted is not food but 'thee', that is God. The move to 'the higher tone' has occurred. The subject praying is anxious to show that he cares much more about Jesus than about food. Another grace in the same primer takes the process a little further:

> Most mightie lord and merciful father we yelde the hartie thanks for our bodely sustenance, requiring also most intirely thi gracious goodness, so to fede

us with the fode of thy hevenly grace that we may worthely gloryfye thy holy name in this life and after be partakers of the life everlasting.

This grace begins, clearly and firmly, with thanks for bodily sustenance, but then the notions of feeding and partaking are abruptly shifted to the spiritual realm and, most important of all, the word 'Grace' in its other signification ('the unmerited generosity of God') breaks in. Grace in this sense was of course the theological obsession of the sixteenth century, and mere 'clang-association' must have made it virtually impossible for them to 'say grace' without mentioning it. Certainly Elizabethan examples abound. The grace said to have been composed about 1565 by one George Bellin, ironmonger of Exeter, reads:

God blesse our meate,
God guide our waies,
God give us grace
Our lord to please.
Lorde long p'serve in peace and health
Our gracious queene Elizabeth.[4]

This would seem to be the proper theological context for the growth of the strange form 'Make us thankful' – as in 'For what we are about to receive may the Lord make us truly thankful' – replacing and undercutting 'We give thanks'. We find it in various Elizabethan graces, for example:

O blessed God and most high kinge
That feedest us evermore;
Give us thy grace that we allwayes
May give thee thankes therefore.[5]

The atmosphere indeed is intensely Protestant. Man can do nothing good of himself; even prayer requires as a precondition the moving, initiating grace of God. It is as if, to modify a phrase of Donne's, the subject must ask separately for 'that Grace to beginne'[6] even in so simple and creaturely an activity as saying grace. Human grace (thanks) requires divine grace (gratuitous favour) before it can start. I have suggested that the final, 'psychologising' twist whereby the giving of thanks becomes instead a petition for thankfulness is essentially Protestant. The fact that Thomas à Kempis, say, before the Reformation prays to be made thankful need not deflect us from this view.[7] Quite apart from the fact that Thomas is notoriously a subjectivist and therefore in a manner a forerunner of Protestant theology, Protestantism itself did not so much invent new doctrines as isolate and heavily emphasise elements which had been present from the beginning. The general, underlying nervousness about the carnality of it all can be found in very early sources. Arnulfus de Boeriis, writing on the religious life (the treatise sometimes known as the *Doctrina Bernardi*) advises his readers to eat little and to bear in mind the fact that Christ expects to be thanked and that meanwhile there is probably a poor man at the gate waiting for the left-overs.[8] Evidently, Arnulfus too is more interested in gratitude than in food. Yet only those keenly interested in food can be truly grateful. One can predict (especially with the help of hindsight) that such people will in time find it impossible to thank God directly for feeding them. Indeed the entire development, which is essentially a transposition from the concrete to the spiritual, is anticipated in the history of the Eucharist itself. 'Eucharist' is in Greek 'thanksgiving' and seems originally to have been linked to the ordinary social eating and drinking of the primitive Christians. But eating and drinking can become uproarious and St Paul it seems was worried. He told the Corinthians to break up their convivial love feasts and to eat and thank God more privately (1 *Corinthians* 11: 22 and 34). It appears that he still wished them to thank God at their meals and to maintain the Eucharist meanwhile as a social ceremony, but the original act was broken and thereby the first move made in separating out the Eucharist. The very retention of the opaque, Greek term in the Western Church where other devotional terms were freely rendered into intelligible Latin is perhaps a mark of an impulse to wrench the spiritual element out of its natural, human context. Had it been translated, the word in English might well have been 'grace'. The mystical doctrine of the Eucharist whereby to eat bread and wine *is* to eat God unifies the carnal and the spiritual, but the unification, it seems, would not hold. The words of the first grace I cited from the King's Primer, 'that in al our meates and drynkes, we may tast and savoure of the' may seem to recover for a moment the original unity of thc Eucharist, but in fact do not. We are conscious of metaphor and therefore of a deliberate displacement in 'tast and savoure'.

There is a story told in E.M. Goulburn's richly Victorian *Office of Holy Communion* of one Fletcher, Vicar of Madeley; he was visited by two friends and became excited on seeing them; when a servant brought in bread and wine, without thinking he broke the bread and passed it to his friends, using the Eucharistic formula. Goulburn, instead of finding this blasphemous as one might expect, comments that it was 'a momentary return to the quite primitive state of things, before the Sacrament was disconnected from the meal'.[9] The piety of the Vicar of Madeley is both eccentrically displaced and strangely fundamental. For an opposite extreme we may turn to the Poet Laureate, Alfred Austin, in whose pages aesthetic young women thank God, not for food nor even for piety but for, of all things, 'serious conversation':

> 'Ought not some one,' said Lamia, as we rose to our feet, 'to say Grace after a meal in this Refectory?' 'Say it then, Lamia,' said Veronica. Lamia bowed her head with deep reverence and at once obeyed, but in a tremulous voice; – 'For these, and all His other mercies, above all for the crowning mercy of serious conversation, God's name be praised!'[10]

Perhaps one more source of sophistication remains. Prayer is, usually, a form of petition addressed to a superior. In such circumstances people are naturally anxious to please and the various elaborations of courteous insinuation gradually infiltrate the form. The third person grammar of the modern grace 'may the Lord make us truly thankful' replacing the traditional second person singular, may be a curious effect of courtliness ('the graces' in Lord Chesterfield's sense!). The second person singular suggests effrontery; hence the transition in so many languages from the intrusive singular to the less importunate plural and then to a still more 'tactful' third person ('Madam' in shops of a certain kind, 'Lei' in Italian).

Timon's lifeless grace plays on these standard paradoxes. The setting must recall to the eye the Last Supper, paradigm of eucharistic feasts.[11] But, here, more savagely than in Buñuel's *Viridiana*, we have not paradigm but a kind of parody. Timon's speech is a web or net of logical and moral *aporiai*, 'bewilderments', and behind the abstraction of the language lie pain and fear. He begins with a high-minded plea for thankfulness, according to the sophisticated mode: 'You great benefactors, sprinkle our society with thankfulness.' But by inserting the word 'society' he insinuates the very different idea of ingratitude between man and man. The following sentence, 'For your own gifts, make yourselves prais'd, but reserve still to give, lest your deities be despised', is thoroughly cynical, but with a streak of madness in it. It offers a 'knowing tip' to the gods to avoid giving, since gifts breed not gratitude but contempt. This is a deliberately muffled version of Lear's trick of projecting his own ills upon the cosmos. But then Timon prays that each person should have enough to make him self-sufficient, enough, in fact, to break the economic nexus of society. By now the high-minded suggestions of the opening sentence are overturned and he asks not for exalted sentiments to fill his heart, but rather for a restoration to that brutalism from which man has fallen away. It is as if the formal development of the grace proper exposes as anomaly in the inner character of courteous gratitude. One cannot thank God for food unless, as Bishop Butler would delight to point out,[12] one values food; but food seems a low business to bring into what may prove an important conversation with the Supreme Being. And thus we see the courtesy of gratitude displacing gratitude itself (the whole meanwhile turning into petitionary prayer of another kind). Timon reverses this process very precisely. Let men, he says, prefer meat to each other.

We have now moved from a plea that society be reformed by being made to learn gratitude to a despair of society and a consequent prayer for its abolition. If all human intercourse is corrupt, the dog that tears its meat is on a higher plane and to that state our piety should henceforth aspire. From here the prayer proceeds by way of the dissolution of meaning to a plea for the destruction of mankind (though the form of words used allows the hearer to assume that only the destruction of sin is intended): 'Let no assembly of twenty be without a score of villains. If there sit twelve women at the table, let a dozen of them be as they are. The rest . . . make suitable for destruction.' In truth, Thanatos here rises in the place of Eros. The score of villains and the twelve bad women are a fool's routine applied with a more than ordinarily destructive intent. The inane tautologies continue to lull the mind (sustaining the 'blah-blah' effect) but at the same time they systematically undo ordered discourse which necessarily involves significant comparison and distinction. The sentence itself mirrors this, beginning with a proposition still formally synthetic, 'Let no assembly of twenty be without a score of villains', but the vacuous equivalence of 'twenty' and 'a score' plants in the mind a ghostly major premiss, 'All men are villains', in which case the proposition is merely analytic, rather like saying, 'if there are twenty people here, there are twenty mortals here'. The analytic and the tautological are near akin and this the sentence finally confesses with the blank nullity of 'as they are'. In a world where all are evil there is no need for the word 'evil'. All are as they are.

The language of Timon's grace is leaden. We miss, at least until the final sentence, the vigour we have come to expect from those who profess to scourge human folly. This is partly because Timon has in fact moved from scourging folly to scourging humanity itself or to a point at which the distinction between fools and human beings can no longer be drawn. He is thus both more radical and more abstract than Apemantus. It is the abstraction from the ordinary vividness of comparative, relational discourse which technically enables the dramatist to keep the speech from impinging too directly on our minds. After all, we are more used to conversing with our own kind; the truly inhuman cannot address us. Yet much is nevertheless said, germane to the whole play.

Timon's onslaught on human relationship works on three interconnected levels, economic, social, and the last a sort of fusion of the logical and ontological. At the beginning of the play he seeks to create a nexus of friendship by giving. One way to understand this sequence is to see it as growing out of *The Merchant of Venice*. In the earlier play Bassanio loves Portia for her beauty, her goodness and her money. His innocently acquisitive ardour is subjected by Shakespeare to an exceptionally subtle species of stylistic mockery. Bassanio is made to apply the traditional allusions to gold and riches, normally metaphors of beauty and virtue, in a wholly literal manner. Portia is a lady 'richly left', suitors seek her as in old time they sought the golden fleece (I. i. 161–72). In all of which Bassanio intends neither more nor less than Portia's enormous fortune. Antonio, meanwhile, loves Bassanio after another manner. His love is not a way of growing rich but a way of emptying his purse and then, perhaps, his veins. Bassanio never gave nor hazarded all he had, but Shylock and Antonio did just that. Merchants are experts, after all, in hazarding. The verbal fencing of Portia and Antonio over the ring (IV. i. 427–54) is also a fencing over Bassanio, who deserves neither of them. Antonio has no chance against biological convention (he is male and Bassanio heterosexual) and he has no chance against enormous wealth; he can only give everything. The conclusion of the comedy miraculously saves his life but does not insult him with a substitute mate. While the rest pair off in the summer night, Antonio is left alone. The drama depends on a presumption of pure altruism in Antonio. He is the unmercenary merchant. The man of bonds and contracts becomes the only giver who secures no just return. This, indeed, would seem to be the essential difference between a mercenary and a loving temper. The first is necessarily reciprocal, the second not.

The proposition is luminous and satisfying, but it did not satisfy the author of *Timon of Athens*. In *Timon of Athens* he does what Shylock was prevented from doing, he rips open the heart of the Giver, to reveal the beating, thirsty interior. Does love really ask for nothing, or is another order of reciprocity and obligation involved? Thus Timon at the beginning of the play has none of Bassanio's cheerful greed. Instead, like Antonio (though in another way, not at all like Antonio) he opens his purse to his friends. It is made very clear that nothing concrete is expected in return. Those who, like Ventidius, offer repayment know that they can rely on Timon's refusal. His bounty offers itself as a non-reciprocal, one-way process.

But *Timon of Athens* is not a comedy but rather a queerly abstract kind of tragedy. The society of the play is neither happy nor good. Those whom Timon loves cannot love others (as Bassanio did). They are *merely* selfish and ungrateful. And in so responding they are breaking not a commercial, but an ethical contract. Timon's bounty was never granted upon legal conditions. There was never any question of repayment. But there was an expectation of love and gratitude in return. They owe him grace for his Grace. That which is gratuitous, by definition, asks for nothing – unless it be gratitude. The terms are cognate, the implied behaviour equally so. Moreover, such an ethical obligation, for all its contempt for the merely commercial contract, can on occasion be translated into cash terms. If a generous man needs money the friend he has helped will give him not just love but also money. Timon, who has given without stint, finds himself pressed hard by creditors and cannot pay. He then expects those he has helped to come to his aid. This is not a mere quirk of his nature but involves an ethically principled claim. Thus we find the language of the contract returning. Feste says in *Twelfth Night* 'Words are very rascals, since bonds disgrac'd them' (III. i. 21), a remark of breathtaking cleverness, since 'disgraced' probably includes, as a subaudition, 'dis-graced', that is 'removed the element of grace and gratitude'. There bonds are the antithesis (as in *The Merchant of Venice*) of a properly human commitment. But in *Timon of Athens* the very notion of a 'bond' is instead extended to the ethical (just as one might have answered Feste, with conscious virtue, '*My* word is my bond!'). When Timon pays Ventidius' debts, the messenger says, 'Your lordship ever *binds* him' (I. i. 107) and Timon explains a gift enabling a servant to marry as fulfilling 'a bond in men' (I. i. 147).

In certain societies, where the convention of an extreme munificence is established, the notion of 'matching' the original liberality – though always distinct from the simple repayment of a debt – can become clearly codified. Because of this implied reciprocity, the receiving of gifts can become as urgently bound up with personal honour as is the dispensing of gifts. Marcel Mauss writes of the American Indians of the North West, 'One does not have the right to refuse a gift or potlatch. To do so would show fear of having to repay.' A little later he adds, interestingly, that 'in certain circumstances, however, a refusal can be an assertion of victory and invincibility'.[13] In Europe we have contrived simultaneously to emphasise the separateness of giving and lending, so that anything which smells of ordinary direct repayment is construed as an insult. Taine tells a story in his *Origines* of the Duc de Richelieu before the French Revolution: he wished his son to learn how to spend like a *grand seigneur* and therefore gave him a purse full of money; the young man brought the money back whereupon the father, by way of paternal instruction, threw the purse out of the window.[14] Of course loans-among-friends can take on some of the moral ambiguities associated with munificence. Thus in certain circumstances a lender can be insulted if it is suggested that he in any way *sought* repayment of a debt. In nineteenth century Russia this could produce extraordinary paroxysms of consideration, especially from debtors like Dostoevsky. Anna, the second wife of the novelist, wrote in her diary, 'As Fyodor owes Turgenev fifty roubles, it is absolutely necessary he should call on him; otherwise Turgenev will think that Fyodor does not want to come out of fear that Turgenev will ask for his money back.'[15] In such webs are we bound.

Timon in the play is subjected to a shock. Even shocks, swift as they are, have a structure and a process. In this play we are admitted to both. To observe the process of Timon's shock is not simply to watch a would-be generous spirit collapsing to become a mercenary spirit. We do not find him out, expose the covertly mercenary character of his seeming generosity. Slick formulae like 'X tries to buy friendship', though undoubtedly relevant to *Timon of Athens* are too coarse, too easy. Timon really did give freely. We have to see that the very freedom with which he gave makes the obligation stronger (even if it is unenforceable in practice) than any obligation imposed by a merely commercial contract. Of course if Timon had originally designed his bounty with the express aim of turning his acquaintances into debtors, that original freedom and altruism would indeed be impaired. But that is not what we are given. Rather he preserves his innocence to the point of shock and then *finds himself surprised* by the selfishness of men.

Innocence of this degree is indeed a kind of stupidity and helps to create the abject behaviour it later finds so shocking, but in all the complex corruption of circumstance the thread of pure generosity may be supposed unbroken. The resulting paradox, that generosity itself entails at the ethical level an obligation of requital, is far more challenging than the cynical, reductive thesis, 'All supposed altruism is really mercenary'. This hunger latent in the superabundance of generosity may be a profound truth of ethics, but to perceive it is to exclude oneself from the ethical. If one knows in advance that one's altruism will demand a return, one cannot be altruistic. Ordinary linguistic idiom seems sometimes to glimpse these truths and then to forget them (cp. 'Mrs Pugh comes in three times a week to oblige', which conventionally raises Mrs Pugh above the merely mercenary though it formally concedes that her behaviour places us under an obligation). The knotty entanglement of generosity with incomprehension on the one hand and reciprocal obligation on the other make it appropriate material for drama, which loves to deal with loss of innocence. But in this case, as we shall see, loss of innocence cannot be followed by enrichment of human nature.

Meanwhile, the obligation entailed in gratitude is also an obligation to give *freely*. This, in the light of what we have said about Timon, may seem merely contradictory. The freedom of Timon's original beneficence depended upon his continuing unawareness that an obligation was being created in the recipient. But the grateful recipient is *ex hypothesi* conscious of obligation. How then can we say that he makes his return *freely*? The freedom here lies in the rule that the return must not be sanctioned by legal or practical force. From the practical point of view the grateful recipient makes his return merely because he wants to, but from the ethical point of view he *ought to want to*. Thus the action remains spontaneous at the level of the practical, but at the level of the ethical the obligation is adamantine. When Flavius, the faithful steward, visits Timon in the wilderness, Timon asks him, wonderingly,

> Is not thy kindness subtle, covetous,
> A usuring kindness, and, as rich men deal gifts,
> Expecting in return twenty for one?
>
> (IV. iii. 512–14)

The analogy is poignant because it is a flawed image of what Timon himself did. He has become half aware that, since he was so shocked by ingratitude, there must have been an unarticulated expectation of reciprocal kindness behind his own giving. But the image is flawed because the expectation was indeed never articulated. The audience, hearing the words, can connect the image of rich men dealing gifts with no one so easily as with Timon himself; but then comes the second stage: this cannot be Timon, for Timon did not give usuriously, for the sake of a return; and then last of all, most fugitive and faint but still soliciting the mind, comes the third thought: 'Yet Timon's giving, if not Timon himself, cried out for a return'. Timon's use of the word 'usuring' is suspended between the commercial and the ethical. The dominant sense is, 'Will you expect money for this?' but behind it we sense the question, 'Will you expect benevolence in return for this?', that is 'Will I be made to break up the perfect protection of my misanthropy because of your goodness?' Within a few lines Timon does both these things: he gives the steward gold and concedes that there is in this corrupt world one honest man.

So far I have argued upwards, from the practical to the ethical, drawing first a contrast (charity, considered practically, is opposed to the world of contracts) and then discovering a structural mirror of the contractual (charity, considered ethically, demands a return). Now we need to redescend to the level of the practical. What is the effect, in practice, of such ethical behaviour? The man who gives freely, even wildly, as Timon does, will not necessarily activate the sense of ethical obligation. Instead he will teach the recipient that he can in fact receive over and over again, with impunity, so to speak. The beneficiaries become like children in an excessively enlightened family where no punishments are ever handed out, betrayed to the crushing liberty of the merely ethical. Once again we find that the apparently gratuitous, non-reciprocal act of giving is in fact entangled in relations, this time of a distressing kind. Political economists used to speak of charity pauperising the recipient. There is a sense in which Timon's almost hysterical insistence on the ethical has morally enslaved his circle of friends. Once again, Timon did not calculate this effect, but his behaviour was calculated to produce it. There is a great sadness here, at the heart of generosity itself, which it is the peculiar merit of this roughly modelled maquette of a play to have seized. His actions *asked* for gratitude, but meanwhile there is the low idiom: he asked for it. The effect of our two levels taken together is that such giving is not, as it purports to be, non-reciprocal, but is on the contrary always reciprocal. Ethically it entails an obligation, practically it invites the non-fulfilment of that obligation. In one sense the ingratitude is formally in accord with the profession of generosity: it takes Timon at his word. Thus we have an exceedingly subtle structure in counterpoint to that surrounding Shylock in *The Merchant of Venice*. Shylock says, in effect, 'You know me; I'm the man who deals not in charity but in strict business terms, and now I want what is owing to me', and the Christians are aghast. In *Timon of Athens* the faithless friends are saying, in effect, to Timon, 'We all know you; you are the one who always gives and to whom we owe nothing', and *he* is aghast.

Aristotle said that the unsocial man was not really a man at all (*Politics* 1253a). Indeed, man's very identity may be constituted by relationships (this feeling is caught perfectly by the triumphant proper noun in Mercutio's words, 'Now art thou sociable, now art thou Romeo!' *Romeo and Juliet* II. iv. 89–90). 'Humanity' is not only a descriptive but also an ethical term. Morality also is fundamentally relational. What Timon finds, or thinks he finds, is that the web of relations is not constitutive of good, but rather of evil. The practical relations parody and betray the ethical. His response is to withdraw, to become a mere unit or monad, windowless, loveless, inhuman. But the play – and language – pursue him even here.

There are, within or above the ordinary web of society, certain special lives, whose significant moments are marked by special terms, commonly borrowed from an older, more august tongue. Thus the life of Christ begins, not just with a birth but with a *Nativity*, and ends with a *Deposition*. Mark Antony and Cleopatra, Plutarch tells us, saw their own superhuman progress as formally divided into the *Amimētobion* ('the Life Inimitable') and the *Synapothanoumenon* ('The Death Together').[16] Timon similarly marks his secession from the human race with a majestic, alien polysyllable: 'I am Misanthropos, and hate mankind.' The unfamiliar word gave the Folio printer some trouble, it seems. He prints '*Misantropos*', italicised with an upper-case swash initial (that is, an elaborately flourished capital letter). When the first form of grace vanished from ordinary human society it turned Greek, became the Eucharist. Timon is a beast–god; *after* his last supper of hatred, he sojourns in the wilderness. Timon's movement into Greek in a manner implies a vanishing, but we still have a word to inform us, even at the limit of language. Timon knows that when he abjures society he also abjures significant introspection, the dialogue of the individual with himself:

> Therefore be abhorr'd
> All feasts, societies and throngs of men!
> His semblable, yea himself, Timon disdains.
> (IV. iii. 20–3)

This warns us that we should look for no enrichment of character in Timon's loss of innocence. He will not, as Richard II did, discover an inward society better than the world's and people his cell with still-breeding thoughts, and in this there is an unavoidable artistic loss. The latter part of *Timon of Athens* cannot enlarge the apprehensions of the audience since it is, in every sense, an excursion into a Waste Land. Therefore the convivial discourse is succeeded by no great tragic soliloquies but rather by a discourse of expletives, petulant, self-destroying. Timon supposes that he can express his vision by inverting ethical categories: 'Black white, foul fair, wrong right' (IV. iii. 29). But, as Blake and Nietzsche were later to find, the transvaluation of values is a systematically impeded thing. If I say that good is bad, what do I mean by 'bad'? Do I use the word in its usual sense? If Timon means only that those who seem loving are not really so, he has done nothing to the structure of *ethics*. If, on the other hand, he means that kindness itself is an evil (for example, because it fosters ingratitude) then indeed he attacks one of the pillars of ethics, but in doing so is forced to defer to one of the other central doctrines, that ingratitude is base. As long as Timon sounds like a traditional *contemptor mundi* (contemner of the world) or satiric scourge of vice he implicitly upholds the fabric of morality. Apemantus cleverly detects the continuing vein of moral principle in Timon when he remarks on his 'slave-like habit' and tells him instead to 'turn rascal' (IV. iii. 205, 217). Timon himself senses that the moralising posture is not appropriate; he must become disgusting, a beast not a man.

As we have seen, references to dogs are poured out in this play. Empson wrote a justly celebrated essay[17] on the curious forms of praise given in *Timon of Athens* to dogs, normally reviled by Shakespeare. The key to the apparent anomaly is, however, really something quite simple. The favour shown to dogs in *Timon* is only a measure of the depth to which man has sunk. It is hardly a compliment to the dog to choose him for this particular purpose. Swift in Part IV of *Gulliver's Travels* brought his hero to a country where the men were bestial and the beasts (horses) humane. Here also the logical mechanism of the satire exposes a state of affairs less radically subversive than we might have supposed. Swift could never have made out his case against the human Yahoos had he not mingled human viciousness with certain simian characteristics, and his rational horses are conversely elevated by certain characteristics which could have been drawn only from the human species in its better moments. For the most radical contrast Swift has only the potent but insufficient fact that human excrement is more disgusting than horse dung. Yet neither Swift nor Gulliver frets at this logical prison as does the author of *Timon*. Indeed *Timon* is an essay in moral logic, at once nightmarish and Euclidian in its procedures, before it is a study of character or temperament. I think it likely that Shakespeare – and perhaps Middleton also – was sufficiently part of the contemporary wave of Tory resentment at the erosion of hospitality and the depredations of usurers to see Timon's original beneficence as authentically noble, even while it is palpably obtuse. The gradual secularisation of solitude chronicled by Janette Dillon is also plainly relevant. But to map these conventions is not enough. Shakespeare always works at the roots, and here, with or without help, he works at the roots of theory.

What Timon finds is that even the mechanism of hatred, even the logic of expletives, remains social. He cannot even hate without presupposing a social logic for his hatred. And if he takes the advice of Apemantus and becomes a rascal he is simply reabsorbed in the convivial texture of a corrupt society. We are made to watch this happen when Timon gives gold to the greedy sycophants who visit him in the wilderness (v. i. 111–14). He seeks to insult them with the gift and yet he gives them what they want. In a manner the necessary friction of misanthropy has gone. Humanity itself is hell, nor is he yet out of it. Apemantus is here once more his teacher:

> Thou shouldst desire to die, being miserable.
>
> (IV. iii. 250)

Timon's grace, with which we began, moved from inversion to the blank insignificance of tautology and thence to the word 'nothing': 'For these my present friends, as they are to me nothing, so in nothing bless them, and to nothing are they welcome.' Timon himself must move from invective through the defeat of language to unbeing. As this process unfolds, the discourse of expletives is played by Shakespeare – and this time I am sure that it is Shakespeare and only he – against a larger poetry, expressive *per impossibile* of this vanishing theme, a poetry of sky and sea. Timon, indeed, sees the heavens themselves as tainted with the corruption of reciprocity:

> . . . the moon's an arrant thief,
> And her pale fire she snatches from the sun;
> The sea's a thief, whose liquid surge resolves
> The moon into salt tears . . .
>
> (IV. iii. 440–3)

But now the poet uses air and sea after another manner, as that which is radically formless, relationless and may therefore stand as a healing icon of the inhuman. We hear this music first when Timon is newly ruined and his household is breaking up; the Third Servant says,

> We must all part
> Into this sea of air.
>
> (IV. ii. 21–2)

Timon himself later says,

> Then, Timon, presently prepare thy grave;
> Lie where the light foam of the sea may beat
> Thy grave-stone daily . . .
>
> (IV. iii. 380–2)

and later still he tells the embassy,

> Come not to me again; but say to Athens,
> Timon hath made his everlasting mansion
> Upon the beached verge of the salt flood,
> Who once a day with his embossed froth
> The turbulent surges shall cover . . .
>
> (V. i. 213–17)

Thus like Canute upon the dark shore of the world, Timon welcomes the overwhelming sea. The hardness of this monument will be eroded by the soft sea-spray and his place of rest will be rocked and swept to and fro in the unsympathising breakers. *Timon of Athens* is indeed Shakespeare's version of what Swift was to do in the last, mind-turning voyage of Lemuel Gulliver.[18] It is, also, with its stream of insults, its reduction of man to the status of a maimed animal in a barren world, Shakespeare's *Endgame*. But the sea-sound, which is to get louder in the last plays, is uniquely Shakespearean, perhaps a kind of grace or benediction after all.

Conclusion
The Two Epitaphs

Timon, most oddly, left behind him not one epitaph but two (or perhaps, as we shall see, three). The soldier who found them took an impression of the inscriptions and carried them to Alcibiades. They are indeed offered as if they were a single memorial:

Sold. My noble general, Timon is dead,
Entomb'd upon the very hem o' th' sea;
And on his grave-stone this insculpture which
With wax I brought away, whose soft impression
Interprets for my poor ignorance.

Alcib. [Reading the Epitaph] *Here lies a wretched corse, of wretched soul bereft:*
Seek not my name. A plague consume you, wicket caitiffs left,
Here lie I, Timon, who, alive, all living men did hate.
Pass by and curse thy fill, but pass and stay not here thy gait.
(v. iv. 65–73)

The relevant passage in North's translation of Plutarch runs as follows:

He died in the city of Hales, and was buried upon the Sea side. Now it chanced so, that the Sea getting in, it compassed his Tomb round about, that no man could come to it: and upon the same was written this Epitaph:

> *Here lies a wretched corse, of wretched soul bereft:*
> *Seek not my name: a plague consume you wicked wretches left.*

It is reported that *Timon* himself, when he lived, made this Epitaph: for that which is commonly rehearsed, was not his, but made by the Poet *Callimachus*:

> *Here lie I,* Timon, *who alive all living men did hate:*
> *Pass by and curse thy fill: but pass and stay not here thy gait.*[1]

It seems that something has gone wrong. To string the two epitaphs together is to transform what in Plutarch is a nice contrast into a simple contradiction, or something very close to contradiction. In Plutarch it is Timon who wraps himself in the oblivion of anonymity and the poet Callimachus who names, for all posterity, the great exemplar of misanthropy. In Shakespeare the epitaph, absurdly, first withholds and then announces Timon's name. It is hard to resist the conclusion of the New Arden editor: that Shakespeare copied from Plutarch (with one minor change) both epitaphs, intending at a later stage to eliminate one of them.

In the text as we have it, Timon seems indeed strangely fertile in producing epitaphs. The Soldier cannot read the inscription because it is in a language unknown to him. This inference is forced on us by the fact that he can and does read the earlier message left behind by Timon, at v. iii. 2:

> Who's here? Speak, ho! No answer? What is this?
> *Timon is dead, who hath outstretch'd his span:*
> *Some beast read this; there does not live a man.*
> Dead, sure; and this his grave.

There is something crazy in the implied picture of a beast solemnly reading a notice (in Lewes cattle market in Sussex, there is a sign which reads, if memory serves, 'Cattle and Calves, Turn Right; Pigs Straight On'). Perhaps the absurdity arises from the conflict of two intentions, one belonging properly to the character, the other authorial. Timon wishes to say that all men are beasts; the author is anxious to stress the act of *reading*, to mark the eerie transition from a living to a legible existence. These words, also, are in some ways like an epitaph, in others like a formal announcement of a death.

Nor is this all. Timon, who after death continues to speak in graven characters, before his death had already begun to assume the accent and cadence of the epitaph:

> . . . say to Athens,
> Timon hath made his everlasting mansion . . .
> (v. i. 213–4)

It is the phrase 'Say to Athens' which seems to come from beyond the grave. What has become in our century the most famous of all Greek epitaphs, that of Simonides for the Spartan dead at Thermopylae, reads as follows:

> *Stranger, tell the Lacedaemonians that we lie*
> *here, having obeyed orders.*[2]

It is as if Timon, as he withdraws from all human conversation, is translated into the public, verbal record of himself; he who was never a man becomes his own unnatural epitaph. The hardness of the inscription, of the stone, is played off against the softness of the wax, which receives the impression, and of the spray which breaks over the gravestone and in like manner the clarity of the memorial loses itself in echoes and pre-echoes. Cleopatra foresees the time when she will be a stock figure of the stage (*Antony and Cleopatra*, v. ii. 220); there at least the secondary existence imagined is one of flesh and blood; Timon becomes mere letters on a stone or a page. We end as we began, with *reading*.

There is a word for this kind of art: *ecphrastic*. An *ecphrasis* in late Greek poetry is a poem which describes a work of art. The term is particularly associated with Paulus Silentiarius and Christodorus who, in the fifth or sixth century AD, wrote a long poem about the statues in the Gymnasium of Zeuxippus. But the term has a usefulness beyond its immediate, technical application. There is a special fascination about poems which pointedly relate not to the world but to images of the world. This fascination is at least as old as the shield of Achilles in Homer and is still strong in Keats's 'Ode on a Grecian Urn' or Auden's 'Musée des Beaux Arts'. In the *Paragone* at the beginning of *Timon* the Poet and the Painter offer competitive *ecphraseis* of their own works. Thereafter we have no technical *ecphrasis*; rather, an ecphrastic atmosphere, in which (especially with Timon himself) we are uncertain whether we are looking at a man or at a simplified picture of a man, is maintained. But there is one great difference. In most powerful ecphrastic poetry there is a tense relation between the coldness of the work of art described and the warmth of life which exists within or beyond it. Commonly the image brightens into life in the course of the poem. Thus in Keats's Ode the figures frozen in marble are gradually freed: the scene takes on colour, the altar to which the priest leads the lowing heifer is not white but green. In the *Iliad* the shield of Achilles bears a scene in gold of men ploughing, yet as they plough the field turns black under the ploughshare (XVIII. 548–9). More elaborately, in *Odyssey* VIII Odysseus at the court of the Phaeacians hears his own story sung by a minstrel; the Phaeacians do not know that he is the great Odysseus; he, listening, weeps at his own history and to hide his tears draws his great purple cloak over his face (84–5). In *Timon* it is otherwise. The ecphrastic image never brightens into life and colour. Instead the seemingly living protagonist dies into the two-dimensional world of incised letters. To say this is to return to what, at the beginning of this essay, I called a 'distinctively Renaissance alienation'. Cyrus Hoy was right to link this play especially to the alienation technique of 'mannerist' art,[3] in which 'violent' perspective effects and distortions of the human body even as they shock us remind us that we are looking at *pictures*.

The catalogue of things *not* done in this play can be further extended – some may think – to a damning extreme. As Timon's period of liberality is unenlivened by any distinct relation of human love, so his sojourn in the wilderness is never fired by any positive affection of a higher order. One has only to see how writers in the earlier, Christian tradition of seclusion express themselves to feel the difference. Take, for example, the English hermit, Richard Rolle (1300–49) on the love of God:

> Love forsooth dwells in the heart of the solitary if he seek nothing from vain lordship. Here he utterly burns and longs for light while he thus clearly savours things heavenly; and sings with honey-sweetness and without heaviness; as the seraphim – to whom he is like in loving mind – cries and says to his noble Lover: 'Behold, loving, I burn; greedily desiring.'[4]

Or Ramon Lull (*c.* 1233–*c.* 1315); 'The Lover longed for solitude, and went away to live alone, that he might gain the companionship of his Beloved, for amid many people he was lonely.'[5] Nor do we find in Timon's sojourn in the wilderness any real imaginative communication of the *wildness* of the place to which he comes, of the dark, pre-moral excitement of going beyond the confines of humanity. Take the marvellous anonymous lyric, 'Loving Mad Tom':

> With an host of furious fancies,
> Whereof I am commander,
> With a burning spear and a horse of air,
> To the wilderness I wander.
> By a knight of ghosts and shadows,
> I summoned am to tourney,
> Ten leagues beyond the wide world's end.
> Methinks it is no journey.[6]

Timon finds in his seclusion no divine lover nor even the high adventure with the faceless Knight of the Unknown.

The consequent impoverishment of both drama and poetry is undeniable. But there is a deeper excitement in this very austerity. Timon, we sense, is *really* alone. Shakespeare is essaying the almost impossible task of dramatising negation itself, and that is why we are given, not a Jacob wrestling with the Angel, but a vanishing figure, lost in water and air, forming at the last not substance but words. In comparison with this severity, we come to see the vividness of 'Loving Mad Tom' or even of the great Christian mystics as a kind of indulgence, a fundamental sentimental domestication of the wilderness, an imaginative refusal to tolerate a world without personal encounter.

All the while this study of an achieved nothingness is structured from within by a powerful philosophic meditation, working through puns, etymology and semantic kinship, on the word *grace*. The implied opposite is *bond*, which teaches us that grace is freedom; freedom may indeed be the most radical idea in the play, linking the original liberality with the ultimate disengagement of the hero. It is characteristic of a term of power, such as *grace* is in this play, that it will generate further punning echoes, beyond those explicitly offered in the text. Thus we may say, following the spirit of the play but without quoting the letter, that it is with an ill grace that Timon offers his Last Supper. We may go further and match *the* alien polysyllable of the text, *Misanthropos*, with one of our own making: Timon's Eucharist is indeed a *Dyscharist*. Meanwhile we, the readers, have in fact been better treated. I began by saying that in this play Shakespeare starves his reader of all the usual good things offered so abundantly in his earlier plays. This may seem to suggest that the parallel with Timon's anti-feast is exact: that, instead of bread, Shakespeare has given us a stone. But the House of Imagination has many rooms. For those who are willing to listen and to learn there is much food in this strange play. It is just not the kind we are used to.

Notes and References

TIMON OF ATHENS
THE STAGE HISTORY

1. See G. Wilson Knight, *Timon of Athens* and its dramatic descendants', *Review of English Literature*, 2 (1961), 9–18. Knight cites a number of more or less analogous works including Cumberland's *The Wheel of Fortune*, whose rashly generous hero was once played by, of all people, the young Lord Byron.
2. See *The New Grove Dictionary of Music and Musicians* edited by Stanley Sadie, 20 vols (London: Macmillan, 1980) vol. xv, p. 469.
3. See C.B. Young's account in J.C. Maxwell (ed.), the New Cambridge edn of *The Life of Timon of Athens* (Cambridge: Cambridge University Press, 1957), p. xlvii.
4. See L.H. and C.W. Houtchens (eds) *Leigh Hunt's Dramatic Criticism, 1808–31* (New York: Columbia University Press, 1949), pp. 138–9.
5. See M.C. Day and J.C. Trewin, *The Shakespeare Memorial Theatre* (London and Toronto: J.M. Dent, 1932), pp. 72–3.
6. G. Wilson Knight, *Shakespeare's Dramatic Challenge: Or the Rise of Shakespeare's Tragic Heroes* (London: Croom Helm, 1977), pp. 163, 165.
7. See Shakespeare, *Timon d'Athènes*, adaption française de Jean-Claude Carrière (Paris: Centre International de Créations Théatrales, 1974) which contains notes on the production and an interview with Peter Brook.

TIMON OF ATHENS
THE CRITICAL RECEPTION

1. *The General Evening Post*, 8–11 February 1772. Brian Vickers believes that the writer was George Steevens. See his *Shakespeare: The Critical Heritage*, vol. v (1979), pp. 487f.
2. Anonymous, ascribed. to Edward Filmer, *A Defence of Dramatick Poetry: Being a Review of Mr Collier's View of the Immorality and Profaneness of the Stage* (1698), in Brian Vickers (ed.), *Shakespeare: The Critical Heritage*, vol. II (1974), p. 90.
3. *Essays on Shakespeare's Dramatic Characters of Richard the Third, King Lear, and Timon of Athens* (1783); in *Shakespeare: The Critical Heritage*, vol. VI (1981), pp. 361, 362–3.
4. Ibid., p. 361.
5. Ibid., vol. v (1979), p. 412.
6. See his *Characters of Shakespeare's Plays* (London: R. Hunter and C. & T. Oliver, 1817), pp. 61–8, esp. pp. 62–3.
7. A.C. Swinburne, *A Study of Shakespeare* (London: Chatto & Windus, 1880), p. 213.
8. See Willard Farnham, *Shakespeare's Tragic Frontier: The World of his Final Tragedies* (Berkeley and Los Angeles: University of California Press, 1950); L.C. Knights, '*Timon of Athens*' in D.W. Jefferson (ed.), *The Morality of Art* (London: Routledge & Kegan Paul, 1969), pp. 1–17; D.A. Traversi, *An Approach to Shakespeare*, 3rd edn, 2 vols (London: Hollis & Carter, 1968–9).
9. *The Origins of Shakespeare* (Oxford: Clarendon Press, 1977), p. 71.

PART 1
THE SUCCESSION OF FIGURES

1. *The Shakespeare First Folio: Its Bibliographical and Textual History* (Oxford: Clarendon Press, 1955), p. 124.
2. Ibid., p. 126.
3. Ibid., p. 125.
4. See Frank Kermode's introductory essay to *Timon of Athens* in *The Riverside Shakespeare*, ed. G. Blakemore Evans *et al.* (Boston: Houghton Mifflin, 1974), p. 1,443.
5. See his probably autobiographical *Somnium* ('A Vision'), 2, in the Oxford Text, *Luciani Opera*, ed. M.D. Macleod (Oxford: Clarendon Press, 1972–), vol. II, pp. 135–6.
6. *Shakespeare's Imagination*, first published 1946 (Lincoln, Nebraska: University of Nebraska Press, 1963), p. 37.
7. 1253a. The English version is that of Ernest Barker (omitting his interpolated. explanatory phrases), from his edition and translation, *The Politics of Aristotle* (first published 1946, London: Oxford University Press, 1958), pp. 5–6.
8. See Diogenes Laertius, *Lives of the Eminent Philosophers*, VI, 13; in the Loeb Classical Library edition with an English translation by W.D. Hicks (London: Heinemann, 1965), vol. II, pp. 12–13.
9. Shakespeare, *Timon of Athens*, ed. H.J. Oliver (London: Methuen, 1963, corrected reprint of 1959 edn, p. xxi.
10. Ibid., p. xxii.
11. London: Charles Knight & Co. See vol. I of the Tragedies, pp. 333–8.
12. E.H. Wright, *The Authorship of Timon of Athens* (New York: Columbia University Press, 1910).
13. 'Shakespeares Timon von Athen', pp. 107–92.
14. F.S. Boas, *Shakespeare and his Predecessors* (London: John Murray, 1896), p. 495. See also ibid., pp. 502–3 where he argues that III. v may well be Shakespearean. K. Deighton agreed with this latter point in his Arden edition of the play (London: Methuen, 1905), p. xix.
15. London: Blackie & Son, 1908, pp. 9–12.
16. *William Shakespeare: A Study of Facts and Problems*, 2 vols (Oxford: Clarendon Press, 1930), vol. I, p. 482.

17. 'Timon of Athens', *Notes and Queries*, 12th Series, 112 (1920), 266–9.
18. 'The problem of *Timon of Athens*', *Notes and Queries*, 13th Series, 5 (1923), 83–6; 6 (1923), 105–7; 7 (1923), 123–6; 8 (1923), 145–9; 9 (1923), 166–8; 10 (1923), 188–90; 11 (1923), 208–10: The argument for Middleton's part in the writing begins in the fourth of these instalments.
19. New York: Columbia University Press, 1955, pp. 218–23.
20. *Op. cit.*, p. 62.
21. Ibid., p. 60.
22.. '*Timon of Athens*', *Shakespeare Quarterly*, 12 (1961), 3–20.
23. *Studies in Attribution: Middleton and Shakespeare* (Salzburg: Universität Salzburg, 1979), p. 64. See also the excellent discussion, in substantial agreement with Jackson, in David J. Lake, *The Canon of Middleton's Plays* (London: Cambridge University Press, 1975), pp. 279–86.
24. See William Wells, '*Timon of Athens*', *Notes and Queries*, 12th Series, 112 (1920), p. 267.
25. *Scenic Form in Shakespeare* (Oxford: Clarendon Press, the corrected issue of 1985), p. 96.
26. *Op. cit.*, p. 63.
27. See his '*Timon of Athens* and the three Graces: Shakespeare's Senecan study', *Modern Philology*, 83 (1985–6), 349–63.
28. *An Itinerary written by F. Moryson, Gent.*, III. iii (London: John Beale, 1617), Sig. Rrrr 2; 4 vols (Glasgow: MacLehose & Sons, 1907–8), vol. IV, p. 169. A facsimile of the 1617 edition is available (New York and Amsterdam: Theatrum Orbis Terrarum, 1971).
29. *The Crisis of the Aristocracy, 1588–1641* (Oxford: Clarendon Press, 1965), p. 528. E.A.J. Honigmann points out in his *Shakespeare: The 'Lost Years'* (Manchester: Manchester University Press, 1985), p. 118, that Shakespeare's father was almost certainly heavily involved in usury.
30. II. i. 17, in *The Works of Middleton*, ed. A.H. Bullen (Boston: Houghton Mifflin, 1885), vol. III, p. 270.
31. See J.W. Draper, 'The theme of *Timon of Athens*', *Modern Language Review*, 29 (1934), 20–31, esp. p. 25.
32. IV. i, in *The Plays and Poems of Richard Brinsley Sheridan*, ed. R. Crompton Rhodes, 3 vols (Oxford: Blackwell, 1928, vol. II, p. 78).
33. J. Pelikan and W.A. Hauser (Saint Louis, Mo: Concordia

Publishing, 1958–) vol. XXVI, 1963, pp. 287–90; in *D. Martin Luthers Werke*, 57 vols (Weimar: specially commissioned, 1883–1921), vol. XL, pp. 448–52.

34. Samuel Johnson, *Lives of the Poets*, ed. G. Birkbeck Hill (Oxford: Clarendon Press, 1905) vol. III, p. 54.
35. *Merit and Responsibility* (Oxford: Clarendon Press, 1960), p. 42.
36. Sir S. Lee, *Life of Shakespeare* (New York: Smith, Elder & Co., 1916), p. 400.
37. See n. 31 *supra*.
38. See *Shakespeare's Library*, ed. W.C. Hazlitt, 6 vols (London: Reeves & Turner, 1875) vol. VI, pp. 393f.
39. Jean de l'Espine, *A Very Excellent and Learned Discourse* (Cambridge, John Legate, 1592), leaf 69, v. This work was translated into English by E. Smyth.
40. S. Rowlands, *The Melancholy Knight* (1615), edited for the Hunterian Club, no. 24 (Glasgow: 1874), p. 7.
41. R. Brathwaite, *The English Gentleman* (London: printed by J. Haviland, sold by R. Bostock, 1630), p. 257. A facsimile of this edition is available (New York and Amsterdam: Theatrum Orbis Terrarum, 1975).
42. Draper, *op. cit.*, p. 22.
43. See Ruth Kelso, *The Doctrine of the English Gentleman in the Sixteenth Century* (Urbana, Illinois: University of Illinois 1929), p. 32.
44. *Worke for Armorours* (1609) in *The Non-Dramatic Works of Thomas Dekker*, 5 vols, ed. A.B. Grosart (New York: Russell & Russell, the 1963 reissue of the edition of 1885), vol. IV, pp. 128f. See also T. Wilson, *Discourse upon Usury*, ed. R.H. Tawney (New York: 1925), pp. 31f.
45. Draper, *op. cit.*, p. 25.
46. See his Essays, *Of Usury* and *Of Expense*, in *The Essayes or Counsels, Civill and Morall*, edited by Michael Kiernan (Oxford: Clarendon Press, 1985), pp. 124–8, 87–8.
47. *A General Discourse against the Damnable Sect of Usurers*, trans. Thomas Rogers (London: John Kyngston for Andrew Maunsell, 1578), p. 7. The first edition of this work appeared in 1569.
48. II. ii, 120–61, in *The Complete Workes of John Lyly*, ed. R.W. Bond (Oxford: Clarendon Press, 1902), vol. II, pp. 332–3.

49. *The Non-Dramatic Works of Thomas Dekker*, ed. A.B. Grosart, vol. II, p. 89.
50. In his translation of Ammianus Marcellinus, *The Roman Historie*, XXII. xi (London: A. Islip, 1609), p. 206.
51. Draper, *op. cit.*, p. 28.
52. Philip Caesar, *A General Discourse against . . . Usurers* (1578); John Wharton, *Whartons Dreame. Conteyninge an invective agaynst certaine abbominable Caterpillers as Usurers . . .* (London: John Charlewood, for P. Conyngton, 1578), leaf 47r; Henry Smith, *The Examination of Usury* (London: R. Field for Thomas Man, 1591), available in facsimile (New York and Amsterdam: Theatrum Orbis Terrarum, 1975); Roger Fenton, *A Treatise of Usurie* (London: Felix Kyngston for William Aspley, 1611), available in facsimile (New York, Amsterdam: Theatrum Orbis Terrarum, 1975); John Blaxton (compiler), *The English Usurer; or Usury condemned, by the most learned and famous Divines of the Church of England*, the second, corrected impression (London: John Morton, to be sold by Francis Bowman, 1634), available in facsimile (New York and Amsterdam: Theatrum Orbis Terrarum, 1974); Miles Mosse, *The Arraignment and Conviction of Usurie* (London: the Widdow Orwin for T. Man, 1595), pp. 101f. See also the various editions of Nicholas Ling, *Polyteuphnia, Wits Commonwealth* (London: James Roberts for N. Ling, 1597 *et seq.*); this work was apparently begun by J. Bodenham.
53. *The Crisis of the Aristocracy*, pp. 750–1.
54. Ibid., pp. 514–15.
55. Ibid., p. 43; Seneca, *De Beneficiis*, VI. iii. 1, in *Seneca: Moral Essays*, with an English translation by J.W. Basore, 3 vols (London: Heinemann, 1928–35) vol. III, p. 366. My attention was drawn to this passage by Emrys Jones.
56. *The Crisis of the Aristocracy*, p. 159.
57. Ibid., p. 339.
58. See R.B. Outhwaite, *Inflation in Tudor and Early Stuart England*, first published 1969, 2nd edition (London: Macmillan, 1982).
59. *Politics*, 1258 a–b, in Ernest Barker's translation, pp. 28–9.
60. See A.S. Collins, '*Timon of Athens*: a reconsideration, *Review of English Studies*, 22 (1946), 96–108, esp. p. 107 and J.C. Maxwell, the New Cambridge edition of *Timon of Athens*, pp. xxxviii–ix.

61. The relevant passage from North's translation is given in the New Arden *Timon of Athens*, p. 141.
62. *Secret History of the Court of James I*, ed. Sir Walter Scott (Edinburgh: J. Ballantyne, 1811), vol. I, pp. 270–1.
63. As John Carey supposes; see his *John Donne: Life, Mind and Art* (London: Faber & Faber, 1981), p. 83.
64. See J.W. Lever, *The Tragedy of State* (London: Methuen, 1971), p. 5.
65. See Sir John Harington's account in E.K. Chambers, *The Elizabethan Stage*, 3 vols (Oxford: Clarendon Press, 1923), vol. I, p. 172n.
66. The speech of Sosicles the Corinthian against Spartan tyranny in Herodotus, *History*, v. 92A.
67. *The Wheel of Fire* (London: Methuen, the 1959 corrected reprint of the enlarged edition of 1949), pp. 207–39.
68. I. ix, in *The Countess of Pembroke's Arcadia*, ed. Maurice Evans (Harmondsworth: Penguin Books, 1977), p. 109.
69. Ibid., p. 109.
70. Ibid., p. 110.
71. Cited in Janette Dillon, *Shakespeare and the Solitary Man* (London: Macmillan, 1981), pp. 25, 31.
72. 'Of solitude', in his *Essays, Plays and Sundry Verses*, ed. A.R. Waller (Cambridge: Cambridge University Press, 1906), p. 394. The Essays were first published in 1668.
73. In the edition by H.H.S. Croft, 2 vols (London: Kegan Paul, Trench & Co., 1883), vol. I, pp. 3–4.
74. *Works*, ed. J. Spedding, R.L. Ellis and D.D. Heath, 14 vols (London: Longman *et al.*, 1857–74), vol. VI, p. 705. See also Dillon, *op. cit.*, p. 29.
75. See *Repentance*, 1592, in *Works*, ed. A.B. Grosart, 12 vols (London: privately printed, 1881–3), vol. XII, p. 172. See also Dillon, *op. cit.*, p. 22.
76. *Pierce Penniless His Supplication to the Devil* (1592), in *The Unfortunate Traveller and Other Works*, ed. J.B. Steane (Harmondsworth: Penguin Books, 1972), p. 64; Dillon, *op. cit.*, p. 31.
77. Dillon, *op. cit.*, pp. 25, 29.
78. Ibid., p. 160.
79. See Diogenes Laertius, *Lives of the Eminent Philosophers*, IX. 61; in the Loeb edition with an English translation by

R.D. Hicks, 2 vols (London: Heinemann, 1925), vol. II, p. 274.

80. *Life of Marcus Antonius*, in the New Arden edition, p. 141.

PART 2
TIMON SAYS GRACE: THE PARODIC EUCHARIST

1. Lib. VIII, caput 49, in J.-P. Migne, *Patrologiae Cursus Completus, Series Graeca*, tom. I (Paris, 1857) col. 1057.
2. I quote from the facsimile reproduction with an introduction by David Siegenthaler, Scholars' Facsimiles and Reprints (New York: Delmer, 1974), no page numbers.
3. See H.L. Dixon, *'Saying Grace' Historically Considered* (Oxford and London: James Parker, 1903), p. 174. The Latin graces of Oxford and Cambridge colleges tend to preserve early forms.
4. Ibid., p. 141.
5. Ibid., p. 143; cp. pp. 142, 155.
6. From the sonnet, 'Oh my blacke Soule!', the second of the 'Divine Meditations' in *The Divine Poems*, ed. Helen Gardner (Oxford: Clarendon Press, 1959), p. 7.
7. *Imitation of Christ*, lib. I, caput 22 (London: Burns Oates, 1933), p. 141.
8. Migne, *Series Latina*, tom. clxxxiv (Paris, 1853) col. 1179.
9. *The Office of Holy Communion in the Book of Common Prayer*, 2 vols (London: Rivingtons, 1863), vol. I, p. 35.
10. *Haunts of Ancient Peace* (London: Adam & Charles Black, 1908), pp. 82–3.
11. Frank Kermode writes on p. 1,443 of his introduction to *Timon of Athens* in *The Riverside Shakespeare*, 'Wilson Knight was obviously justified in staging the banquet scenes (I. ii, III. vi) so that they resembled the Last Supper of the painters.'
12. '. . . all particular appetites and passions are *towards external things themselves*, distinct from the *pleasure arising from them* . . .'; '. . . if by covetousness is meant a desire and pursuit of riches for their own sake, without any regard to, or consideration of, the uses of them; this hath as little

to do with self-love, as benevolence hath', Sermon XI, in *The Analogy of Religion . . . and Fifteen Sermons* (London: George Bell, 1897), pp. 486 and 494.
13. *The Gift: Forms and Functions of Exchange in Archaic Societies*, trans. I. Cunnison (London: Cohen & West, 1954), p. 39.
14. H. Taine, *Les Origines de la Civilisation française, l'Ancien Régime*, II. ii. 2, in the translation by John Durand, *The Ancient Régime* (London: Daldy, Isbister & Co., 1876), p. 131. See also N. Elias, *The Court Society*, trans. E. Jephcott (Oxford: Blackwell, 1983), p. 67.
15. Quoted in E.H. Carr, *Dostoevsky, 1821–1881* (London: Allen & Unwin, 1962), pp. 133–4.
16. Plutarch, *Lives of the Noble Grecians and Romans*, trans. Sir Thomas North, the 1967 reissue by AMS Press Inc., New York, of the 1896 London edn, with an introduction by George Wyndham, vol. VI, pp. 27, 75.
17. 'Timon's dog', in his *The Structure of Complex Words* (London: Chatto & Windus, 1953), pp. 175–84.
18. See John W. Draper, 'The theme of *Timon of Athens*', *Modern Language Review*, 29 (1934), p. 28.

CONCLUSION
THE TWO EPITAPHS

1. See the New Arden edition, p. 142.
2. No. 212 in *The Oxford Book of Greek Verse*, chosen by Gilbert Murray, Cyril Bailey, E.A. Barber, T.F. Higham and C.M. Bowra (Oxford: Clarendon Press, 1946).
3. 'Jacobean tragedy and the mannerist style', *Shakespeare Survey*, 26 (1973), 49–67, esp. pp. 58–60.
4. *The Fire of Love, or the Melody of Love and the Mending of Life*, XIV, trans. Frances M.M. Comper (London: Methuen, 1914), p. 65.
5. *The Book of the Lover and the Beloved*, 45, trans. E. Allison Peers (London: SPCK, 1923), p. 31.
6. *The New Oxford Book of English Verse*, chosen and edited

by Helen Gardner (London: Oxford University Press, 1972), p. 371. Robert Graves thought this stanza was by Shakespeare and closely related to *King Lear*; see his *The Crowning Privilege* (Harmondsworth: Penguin Books, 1959), pp. 265–6.

Select Bibliography

Adkins, A.W.H., *Merit and Responsibility* (Oxford: Clarendon Press, 1960).

Alexander, Peter, *Shakespeare's Life and Art* (London: J. Nisbet, 1939).

Apostolical Constitutions, in J.-P. Migne (ed.), *Patrologiae Cursus Completus*, Series Graeca, 161 vols (Paris, 1857–66), vol. 1 (1857), cols 509–1156.

Aristotle, *The Politics of Aristotle*, ed. and trans. Ernest Barker, first published 1946 (London: Oxford University Press, 1958).

Armstrong, Edward A., *Shakespeare's Imagination*, first published 1946 (Lincoln, Nebraska: University of Nebraska Press, 1963).

Arnulfus de Boeriis, *Documenta Vitae Religiosae* (otherwise known as the *Doctrina Bernardi*), in J-P. Migne (ed.), *Patrologiae Cursus Completus*, Series Latina, 221 vols (Paris, 1844–64), vol. 184 (1859), cols 1178–82.

Augustine, *Enchiridion*, in J.-P. Migne (ed.), *Patrologiae Cursus Completus*, Series Latina, vol. 40 (1861), cols 231–90.

Austin, Alfred, *Haunts of Ancient Peace* (London: Adam & Charles Black, 1908).

Bacon, Francis, *The Essayes or Counsells, Civill and Morall*, ed. Michael Kiernan (Oxford: Clarendon Press, 1985).

Bacon, Francis, *The Works of Francis Bacon*, eds James Spedding, R.L. Ellis and D.D. Heath, 14 vols (London: Longman, 1857–74).

Bergeron, David M., '*Timon of Athens* and morality drama', *College Language Association Journal*, 10 (1967), 181–8.

Blaxton, John (compiler), *The English Usurer; or Usury condemned by the most learned and famous Divines of the Church of England*, the second, corrected impression (London: John Morton, to be sold by Francis Bowman, 1634); available in facsimile (New York and Amsterdam: Theatrum Orbis Terrarum, 1974).

Boas, F.S., *Shakespeare and his Predecessors* (London: John Murray, 1896).

Bonnard, G.A., 'Note sur les sources de *Timon of Athens*', *Études Anglaises*, 7 (1954), 39–69.

Bradbrook, M.C., '*The Comedy of Timon*: a reveling play of the Inner Temple', *Renaissance Drama*, 9 (1966), 83–103.

Bradbrook, M.C., 'Blackfriars: the pageant of *Timon of Athens*', in her *Shakespeare the Craftsman* (Cambridge: Cambridge University Press, 1969), pp. 144–67.

Brathwaite, R., *The English Gentleman* (London: printed by J. Haviland, sold by R. Bostock, 1630); available in facsimile (New York and Amsterdam: Theatrum Orbis Terrarum, 1975).

Brownlow, F.W., *Two Shakespearean Sequences* (London: Macmillan, 1977), esp. pp. 216–32.

Bullough, Geoffrey (ed.), *Narrative and Dramatic Sources of Shakespeare*, 8 vols (London: Routledge & Kegan Paul; New York: Columbia University Press, 1957–75).

Butler, Francelia, *The Strange Critical Fortunes of Shakespeare's Timon of Athens* (Ames, Iowa: Iowa State University Press, 1966).

Butler, Joseph, *The Analogy of Religion . . . and Fifteen Sermons* (London: George Bell, 1897).

Caesar, Philip, *A General discourse against the Damnable Sect of Usurers*, trans. Thomas Rogers (John Kyngston for Andrew Maunsell, London, 1578).

Campbell, O.J., *Shakespeare's Satire* (London: Oxford University Press, 1943).

Carey, John, *John Donne: Life, Mind and Art* (London: Faber & Faber, 1981).

Carr, E.H., *Dostoevsky, 1821–1881* (London: Allen & Unwin, 1962).

Chambers, E.K., *The Elizabethan Stage*, 3 vols (Oxford: Clarendon Press, 1923).

Chambers, E.K., *William Shakespeare: A Study of Facts and*

Problems, 2 vols (Oxford: Clarendon Press, 1930).

Chaucer, Geoffrey, *The Complete Works of Geoffrey Chaucer*, ed F.N. Robinson (Boston: Houghton Mifflin, 1933).

Clemen, W.H., *The Development of Shakespeare's Imagery* (London: Methuen, 1951).

Collins, A.S., '*Timon of Athens: a reconsideration*', *Review of English Studies*, 22 (1946), 96–108.

Cook, David, '*Timon of Athens*', *Shakespeare Survey*, 16 (1963), 84.

Cowley, Abraham, *Essays, Plays and Sundry Verses*, ed. A.R. Waller (Cambridge: Cambridge University Press, 1906).

Day, M.C. and Trewin, J.C., *The Shakespeare Memorial Theatre* (London and Toronto: J.M. Dent, 1932).

Dekker, Thomas, *The Non-dramatic Works of Thomas Dekker*, ed. A.B. Grosart, 5 vols (New York: Russell & Russell, the 1963 reissue of the edition of 1884–6).

De l'Espine, Jean, *A Very Excellent and Learned Discourse* (Cambridge: John Legate, 1592).

Dillon, Janette, *Shakespeare and the Solitary Man* (London: Macmillan, 1981).

Diogenes Laertius, *Lives of the Eminent Philosophers*, with an English translation by R.D. Hicks, the Loeb Classical Library, 2 vols (London: Heinemann, 1959).

Dixon, H.L., *'Saying Grace' Historically Considered* (Oxford and London: James Parker, 1903).

Donne, John, *The Divine Poems*, ed. Helen Gardner (Oxford: Clarendon Press, 1959).

Draper, John W., 'The theme of *Timon of Athens*', *Modern Language Review*, 29 (1934), 20–31.

Dugdale-Sykes, H., 'The problem of *Timon of Athens*', *Notes and Queries*, 13th series, 5 (1923), 83–6; 6 (1923), 105–7; 7 (1923), 123–6; 8 (1923), 145–9; 9 (1923), 166–8; 10 (1923), 188–90; 11 (1923), 208–10.

Edwards, Philip W., *Shakespeare and the Confines of Art* (London: Methuen, 1968).

Elias, N., *The Court Society*, trans. E. Jephcott (Oxford: Blackwell, 1983).

Ellis-Fermor, Una, '*Timon of Athens*: an unfinished play', *Review of English Studies*, 18 (1942), 270–83. Also available in *Shakespeare the Dramatist*, ed. Kenneth Muir (London: Methuen, 1961).

Elyot, Sir Thomas, *The Boke named the Governour*, ed. H.H.S.S. Croft, 2 vols (London: Kegan Paul, Trench, 1883).

Empson, William, *The Structure of Complex Words* (London: Chatto & Windus, 1953).

Farnham, Willard, *Shakespeare's Tragic Frontier: The World of his Final Tragedies* (Berkeley and Los Angeles: University of California Press, 1950).

Fenton, Roger, *A Treatise of Usurie* (Felix Kyngston for William Aspley, 1611); available in facsimile (New York and Amsterdam: Theatrum Orbis Terrarum, 1975).

Gardner, Helen (ed.), *The New Oxford Book of English Verse* (London: Oxford University Press, 1972).

Goulburn, E.M., *The Office of Holy Communion in the Book of Common Prayer*, 2 vols (London: Rivington, 1863).

Graves, Robert, *The Crowning Privilege* (Harmondsworth: Penguin, 1959).

Greene, Robert, *The Life and Complete Works, in prose and verse, of Robert Greene*, ed. A.B. Grosart, 15 vols (London and Aylesbury: privately printed, 1881–6).

Greg, W.W., *The Shakespeare First Folio: Its Bibliographical and Textual History* (Oxford: Clarendon Press, 1955).

Grove, Sir George. See under Sadie, Stanley.

Hazlitt, W.C. (ed.), *Shakespeare's Library*, 6 vols (London: Reeves & Turner, 1875).

Hazlitt, William, *Characters of Shakespeare's Plays* (London: R. Hunter & C. and J. Oliver, 1817).

Henry VIII, *The Primer set furth by the Kinges Majestie & his Clergie*, 1545, facsimile reproduction with introduction by David Siegenthaler, Scholars' Facsimiles and Reprints (New York: Delmer, 1974).

Holland, Philemon, *The Roman Historie* [of Ammianus Marcellinus] (London: A. Islip, 1609).

Honigmann, E.A.J., *The Stability of Shakespeare's Text* (London: Edward Arnold, 1965).

Honigmann, E.A.J., '*Timon of Athens*', *Shakespeare Quarterly*, 12 (1961), 3–20.

Hoy, Cyrus, 'Jacobean tragedy and the mannerist style', *Shakespeare Survey*, 26 (1973), 49–67.

Hunt, Leigh, *Leigh Hunt's Dramatic Criticism*, ed. L.H. and C.W. Houtchens (New York: Columbia University Press, 1949).

Hunter, G.K., 'The last tragic heroes', in *Later Shakespeare*, Stratford-upon-Avon Studies, 8, ed. John Russell Brown and Bernard Harris (London: Edward Arnold, 1966), pp. 11–28.

Jackson, MacDonald P., *Studies in Attribution: Middleton and Shakespeare* (Salzburg: Universität Salzburg, 1979).

Johnson, Samuel, *Lives of the English Poets*, 3 vols, ed. G. Birkbeck Hill (Oxford: Clarendon Press, 1905).

Johnson, Samuel, *Dr. Johnson on Shakespeare*, ed. W.K. Wimsatt, Penguin Shakespeare Library (Harmondsworth: Penguin, 1969), pp. 127–8.

Jones, Emrys, *The Origins of Shakespeare* (Oxford: Clarendon Press, 1977).

Jonson, Ben, *Ben Jonson*, ed. C.H. Herford and Percy and Evelyn Simpson, 11 vols (Oxford: Clarendon Press, 1925–52).

Kelso, Ruth, *The Doctrine of the English Gentleman in the Sixteenth Century* (Urbana, Illinois: University of Illinois, 1929).

Kempis, Thomas à, *Imitation of Christ* (London: Burns Oates, 1933).

Knight, G. Wilson, *Shakespeare's Dramatic Challenge: On the Rise of Shakespeare's Tragic Heroes* (London: Croom Helm, 1977), esp. pp. 147–66.

Knight, G. Wilson, '*Timon of Athens* and Buddhism', *Essays in Criticism* 30 (1980), 105–23.

Knight, G. Wilson, '*Timon of Athens* and its dramatic descendants', *Review of English Literature*, 2 (1961), 9–18.

Knight, G. Wilson, *The Wheel of Fire: Essays in interpretation of Shakespeare's Sombre Tragedies* (London: Oxford University Press, 1930, reprinted 1960).

Knights, L.C., '*Timon of Athens*' in *The Morality of Art*, ed. D.W. Jefferson (London: Routledge & Kegan Paul, 1969), pp. 1–17.

Lake, David J., *The Canon of Middleton's Plays* (London: Cambridge University Press, 1975).

Lancashire, Anne, '*Timon of Athens*: Shakespeare's *Dr. Faustus*', *Shakespeare Quarterly*, 21 (1970), 35–44.

Lee, Sir S., *Life of Shakespeare* (New York: Smith, Elder & Co., 1916).

Lever, J.W., *The Tragedy of State* (London: Methuen, 1971).

Levitsky, Ruth, '*Timon*, Shakespeare's *Magnyfycence* and an embryonic *Lear*', *Shakespeare Studies*, 11 (1978), 107–21.

Ling, Nicholas, *Polyteuphnia, Wits Commonwealth* (London: James Roberts for N. Ling, 1597). This work was apparently begun by J. Boderham.

Lombardo, Agostino, 'The two Utopias of *Timon of Athens*', *Shakespeare Jahrbuch*, 120 (1984), 85.

Lucian, *Luciani Opera*, 3 vols, ed M.D. Macleod (Oxford: Clarendon Press, 1972–80).

Lull, Ramon, *The Book of the Lover and the Beloved*, trans. E. Allison Peers (London: SPCK, 1923).

Luther, Martin, *D. Martin Luthers Werke*, 57 vols (Weimar: specially commissioned, 1883–1921).

Luther, Martin, *Luther's Works*, ed and trans. J. Pelikan and W.A. Hauser (Saint Louis, Mo.: Concordia Publishing, 1958–).

Lyly, John, *The Complete Works of John Lyly*, ed R.W. Bond, 3 vols (Oxford: Clarendon Press, 1902).

Mauss, Marcel, *The Gift: Forms and Functions of Exchange in Archaic Societies*, trans. I. Cunnison (London: Cohen and West, 1954).

Merchant, W.M., '*Timon* and the conceit of art', *Shakespeare Quarterly*, 6 (1955), 250.

Middleton, Thomas, *The Works of Middleton*, ed. A.H. Bullen (Boston: Houghton Mifflin, 1885).

Miola, Robert S., 'Timon in Shakespeare's Athens', *Shakespeare Quarterly*, 31 (1980), 23, 30.

Moryson, F., *An Itinerary*, 4 vols (Glasgow: MacLehose and Sons, 1907–8).

Moryson, F., *An Itinerary written by F. Moryson, Gent.*, a facsimile of the 1617 edn (New York and Amsterdam: Theatrum Orbis Terrarum, 1971).

Mosse, Miles, *The Arraignment and Conviction of Usurie* (London: the Widdow Orwin for Thomas Man, 1595).

Muir, Kenneth, '*Timon of Athens* and the cash-nexus', *Modern Quarterly Misc.*, 1 (1947), 57–76.

Murray, Gilbert, Bailey, Cyril, Barber, E.A., Higham, T.F. and Bowra, C.M., eds, *The Oxford Book of Greek Verse*

(Oxford: Clarendon Press, 1946).

Nashe, Thomas, *The Unfortunate Traveller and Other Works*, ed. J.B. Steane (Harmondsworth: Penguin Books, 1972).

Nowottny, Winifred M.T., 'Acts IV and V of *Timon of Athens*', *Shakespeare Quarterly*, 10 (1959), 496.

Outhwaite, R.B., *Inflation in Tudor and Early Stuart England*, first published 1969, 2nd edn (London: Macmillan, 1982).

Parrott, T.M., *The Problem of Timon of Athens* (London: *Shakespeare Association Papers*, no. 10, 1923).

Pasco, Richard, '*Timon of Athens*', in *Players of Shakespeare*, ed. Philip Brockbank (Cambridge: Cambridge University Press, 1985), pp. 129–38.

Pettet, E.C., '*Timon of Athens*: the disruption of feudal morality', *Review of English Studies*, 23 (1947), 321–36.

Plutarch, *Lives of his Noble Grecians and Romans*, trans. Sir Thomas North, 2 vols (the 1967 reissue by AMS Press, Inc., New York of the 1895 London edn, with an introduction by George Wyndham).

Ramsey, Jarold W., 'Timon's Imitation of Christ', *Shakespeare Studies*, 2 (1966), 162–73.

Richardson, William, *Essays on Shakespeare's Dramatic Characters* (London: John Murray, 1783). Some copies of this book are dated 1784.

Rolle, Richard, *The Fire of Love, or the Melody of Love and the Mending of Life*, trans. Frances M.M. Comper (London: Methuen, 1914).

Rowlands, S., *The Melancholy Knight* (1615), edited for the Hunterian Club, no. 24 (Glasgow, 1874).

Sadie, Stanley (ed.), *The New Grove Dictionary of Music and Musicians*, 20 vols (London: Macmillan, 1980).

Schoenbaum, Samuel, *Middleton's Tragedies* (New York: Columbia University Press, 1955).

Scott, Sir Walter (ed.), *Secret History of the Court of James I*, (Edinburgh: J. Ballantyne, 1811).

Scott, William O., 'The paradox of Timon's self-cursing', *Shakespeare Quarterly*, 35 (1984), 290–304.

Seneca, Lucius Annaeus, *Moral Essays*, with an English translation by J.W. Basore, 3 vols (London: Heinemann, 1928–35).

Shakespeare, William, *The Pictorial Shakespeare*, ed. Charles Knight (London: Charles Knight, 1838).

Shakespeare, William, *The Riverside Shakespeare* (Boston: Houghton Mifflin, 1974).

Shakespeare, William, *Timon d'Athènes*, adaptation française de Jean-Claude Carrière (Paris: Centre International de Créations Théatrales, 1974).

Shakespeare, William, *Timon of Athens*, ed. K. Deighton (London: Methuen, 1905).

Shakespeare, William, *Timon of Athens*, ed. G.R. Hibbard (Harmondsworth: Penguin, 1970).

Shakespeare, William, *Timon of Athens*, the New Cambridge edition by J.C. Maxwell (Cambridge: Cambridge University Press, 1957).

Shakespeare, William, *Timon of Athens*, the New Arden edition by H.J. Oliver (London: Methuen, 1963, corrected reprint of the 1959 edn).

Shakespeare, William, *Works* the Red Letter edition (London: Blackie, 1908).

Sheridan, R.B., *The Plays and Poems of Richard Brinsley Sheridan*, ed. R. Crompton Rhodes, 3 vols (Oxford: Blackwell, 1928).

Sidney, Sir Philip, *The Countess of Pembroke's Arcadia*, ed. Maurice Evans (Harmondsworth: Penguin, 1977).

Sisson, C.J., *New Readings in Shakespeare*, 2 vols (Cambridge: Cambridge University Press, 1956).

Slights, William W.E., '*Genera Mixta* and *Timon of Athens*', *Studies in Philology*, 74 (1977), 61.

Smith, Henry, *The Examination of Usury* (London: R. Field for Thomas Man, 1591); available in facsimile (New York and Amsterdam: Theatrum Orbis Terrarum, 1975).

Soellner, Rolf, *Timon of Athens: Shakespeare's Pessimistic Tragedy* (Columbus, Ohio: Ohio State University Press, 1979).

Spencer, T.J.B. '"Greeks" and "Merrygreeks": a background to *Timon of Athens* and *Troilus and Cressida*', in *Essays on Shakespeare and Elizabethan Drama*, ed. Richard Hosley (London: Routledge & Kegan Paul, 1963), pp. 223–33.

Spencer, T.J.B., 'Shakespeare learns the value of money', *Shakespeare Survey*, 6 (1953), 115–35.

Stone, Lawrence, *The Crisis of the Aristocracy, 1588–1641.* (Oxford: Clarendon Press, 1965).

Swinburne, Algernon Charles, *A Study of Shakespeare* (London: Chatto & Windus, 1880).

Taine, H., *Les Origines de la Civilisation française, l'Ancien Régime*, trans. John Durand as *The Ancient Régime* (London: Daldy, Isbister & Co.: 1876).

Traversi, Derek Antony, *An Approach to Shakespeare*, 3rd edn, 2 vols (London: Hollis and Carter, 1968–9).

Vickers, Brian (ed.), *Shakespeare: The Critical Heritage*, 6 vols (Boston and London: Routledge & Kegan Paul, 1974–81).

Walker, Lewis, '*Timon of Athens* and the Morality tradition', *Shakespeare Studies*, 12 (1979), 159–77.

Wallace, John M., '*Timon of Athens* and the three Graces: Shakespeare's Senecan study', *Modern Philology*, 83 (1985–6), 349–63.

Wells, William, '*Timon of Athens*', *Notes and Queries*, 12th series, 112 (1920), 266–9.

Wendlandt, W., 'Shakespeare's *Timon von Athen*', *Shakespeare Jahrbuch*, 23 (1888), 107–92.

Wharton, John, *Whartons Dreame: Conteyninge an invective agaynst certaine abbominable Caterpillers as Usrers* (London: John Charlewood, for P. Conyngton, 1578).

Whiter, Walter, *A Specimen of a Commentary on Shakespeare* (1794), eds Alan Over and Mary Bell (London: Methuen, 1967).

Wilson, Harold S., *On the Design of Shakespearean Tragedy* (Toronto: University of Toronto Press, 1957).

Wilson, E.H., *Discourse upon Usury*, ed. R.H. Tawney (London: G. Bell & Sons, 1925).

Wright, E.H., *The Authorship of Timon of Athens* (New York: Columbia University Press, 1910).

Index